Apparel Costing

Apparel Costing

Andrea Kennedy, Andrea Reyes,
and Francesco Venezia

BLOOMSBURY VISUAL ARTS
LONDON • NEW YORK • OXFORD • NEW DELHI • SYDNEY

BLOOMSBURY VISUAL ARTS
Bloomsbury Publishing Plc
50 Bedford Square, London, WC1B 3DP, UK
1385 Broadway, New York, NY 10018, USA

BLOOMSBURY, BLOOMSBURY VISUAL ARTS and the Diana logo are trademarks of Bloomsbury Publishing Plc

First published in Great Britain 2020

A catalogue record for this book is available from the British Library.

Library of Congress Cataloging-in-Publication Data
Names: Kennedy, Andrea (Assistant professor of fashion merchandising), author.
Title: Apparel costing / Andrea Kennedy, Andrea Reyes and Francesco Venezia.
Description: London; New York: Bloomsbury Visual Arts, 2020. | Includes bibliographical
references and index.
Identifiers: LCCN 2019037357 (print) | LCCN 2019037358 (ebook) | ISBN 9781350065413 (HB) |
ISBN 9781350065406 (PB) | ISBN 9781350065420 (ePDF)
Subjects: LCSH: Clothing trade–Accounting. | Clothing trade–Costs.
Classification: LCC HF5686.C44 K36 2019 (print) | LCC HF5686.C44 (ebook) | DDC 687.068/1–dc23
LC record available at https://lccn.loc.gov/2019037357
LC ebook record available at https://lccn.loc.gov/2019037358

ISBN: HB: 978-1-3500-6541-3
PB: 978-1-3500-6540-6
ePDF: 978-1-3500-6542-0
eBook: 978-1-3501-9700-8

Typeset by Deanta Global Publishing Services, Chennai, India

To find out more about our authors and books visit www.bloomsbury.com and
sign up for our newsletters.

Contents

Acknowledgments

We extend our deep appreciation and many thanks to those amazing industry professionals, colleagues, and friends who so generously provided knowledge, costing information, confirmed details, and helped in so many various ways along the way.

All our thanks and gratitude go to

- Binson Shrethsa: Co-Founder of Stemp Apparel, maker of clothing and accessories from hemp. Please check out Benson's wonderfully-sustainable line https://www.stempnyc.com/.

- Daniella Ambrogi: Vice President Marketing at Lectra or follow the QR code. Please contact Daniella to learn all about Lectra's end-to-end PD, Cutting, Marking On-Demand Manufacturing software programs at d.ambrogi@lectra.com.

- Edie Roberts: Founder of Edie Inc and Design Director at Edie@Home and Levinsohn Textile Company. Please look for the Edie@Home pillow line at many online retailers.

- Elizabeth Pape: Founder of clothing label Elizabeth Suzann, for granting the permission of her SMOCK cost-breakdown sketch, placed in Chapter 4. Please check out her fabulous line designed and made in Nashville!

- Juliette Atwi: Adjunct Professor at LIM College and product development and supply chain extraordinaire!

- Kenneth Blum: Northeastern Brokerage Company, headquartered right at JFK Airport. Visit Northeastern at http://www.necb.net/ or follow the QR code, for all your freight forwarding needs.

- Sergio Prusky: InStyle Software and InStyle PLM. Please contact Sergio for PLM program information at sergio@instylesoft.com.

- Melissa Rusinek: MS, Environmental Management and Sustainability—Blockchain technology reference.

- Anthony Cibelli: Top Notch Pattern INC. NYC-based grading and marking services.

Preface

The fashion industry is an ever-changing and exciting industry, where nothing stands still. Trends, fabrics, colors, silhouettes, and styling seem to change by the day. Technology and how it impacts sourcing, production timelines, and supply chain models are constantly evolving to help companies remain competitive. The marketing strategies for customers and distribution channels are shifting to nimbler models. Just as every change impacts the apparel industry as a whole, every change must impact apparel costing methods as well. Designers and merchandisers must balance quality, price, and profit (the amount of money gained; the difference between the amount spent and earned after selling), while often also revising their current practices. Companies must consider their current and the changing strategies in design, development, sourcing, production, marketing, and distribution, and tweak their costing methods to adapt to each change accordingly.

Apparel Costing details traditional and current costing methods as well as costing for today's (and tomorrow's) global, fast-paced, e-commerce–focused, slowly becoming more sustainable fashion marketplace. It provides readers with the components, information, and sample cost sheets needed for garment and sewn-product costing and pricing in today's market. Students will learn that so often young designers, companies, and newcomers to the fashion industry (like themselves) formulate costing on the sum of the costs of a style's fabric, trims, and labor—and to that they add their markup. However, every other activity of their business erodes at that markup, and they find themselves with an unsustainable profit—or at a loss. This book offers guidance to help ensure that all cost factors, for a variety of supply chains, are included to guarantee a sustainable profit.

You will learn industry-specific costing that can be applied to products produced both locally and globally. The factors addressed are needed for profit-driven costing, including how to calculate line item percentages on indirect cost factors. Such factors are factory sourcing, overhead, administration, and product development. You will also gain current knowledge of pricing and costing strategies for today's industry. Additionally, as our industry moves toward a more ethically-responsible supply chain, we will compare how cost is calculated in the present to the ways costs should be calculated in the future, with a focus on socially-responsible and transparent production.

This book includes the collective knowledge gained over many years of costing and design meetings, as well as the many years consulting with designers and product development teams. There are all types of costing styles, from custom-made, one-of-a-kind pieces to large-batch styles. No matter the scale of the business, we must make sure we leave nothing out of our cost sheet. Otherwise, we inadvertently take away from our profitability.

Thank you,
Andrea Kennedy, Andrea Reyes, Francesco Venezia, New York

Introduction

Companies are questioning their costing now more than ever. Why do you think that is? It is not because they do not know how to cost. Most companies know how to utilize costing. They have been costing quite well for years. They are experts at costing. However, in this ever-changing fashion world, even the most seasoned fashion professionals cannot continue to cost the same way as they always have. In the current retail environment, many retailers are discounting merchandise, almost on a continual basis. This has caused an increase in **discounts**, **chargebacks**, and **markdowns**, and a decline in **profit** for all. Chargebacks are the percent or dollar amount deducted by the retailer/vendor from the retailers discounted merchandise when the merchandise is unable to be sold at full price, due to receiving the product incomplete, late, or damaged, or if the product is simply not found desirable by the customer. This increase in chargebacks and markdowns has resulted in a decline in profit for all.

Manufacturers and private label retailers alike, who have been professionally costing for years, are suddenly finding themselves with decreased same-store sales figures for several consecutive months. And why is that? Stores are over-stocked with merchandise and the average consumer is seeking the least-expensive option. The ways in which consumers shop is constantly changing—via more e-commerce sites, mobile shopping, same-day or next-day delivery, and more automation in stores. At the same time, the way apparel businesses manufacture goods is evolving. Thanks to CAD, CAM, 3-D and PLM technology, many designs, sourcing, and production steps are now digital, and our garments are produced quicker and cheaper than ever before. The software and automated equipment has a high cost but allows for increased productivity, and therefore increased sales.

Increased sales generally equal increased profits. But this is not the case currently. The recent drop in profits for all the stakeholders—retailers, manufacturers, and factories—is a concern for all, and costing is a factor that is first analyzed. In most instances, solely focusing on costing will not solve the problem of declining profits. Companies must analyze everything from their styling, fit, fabrication, timing, merchandising, production, retail locations, marketing methods, and consumer values concerns.

Most importantly, businesses should be concerned with their corporate cultures within their companies. If a few of these factors are out-of-date, no matter the sharpness in costing and pricing, a company will not be profitable. Nevertheless, most companies look first at their cost sheets. It is much easier to revise a cost sheet than change your fit standards or production methods. In looking first at costing, it is important to ensure that every expense of business is accounted for within a cost sheet.

Generally, before looking at costing-per style, a company first looks at their **income statement** (Table 0.1). The income statement shows a company's financial performance over the year, quarter, or other specified periods of time. A company will first look at the **top line,** the gross sales or revenue of their company, then they look at the **bottom line**, their net profit or loss. The bottom line is the most important

Table 0.1 Example of a basic income statement

ABC Apparel Inc. Income Statement		
Gross Sales	1,000,000	TOP LINE
– Sales Returns	–20,000	
Net Sales	980,000	
– Cost of Goods Sold (COGS)	–500,000	
Gross Profit	480,000	
Operating Expenses (administration, utilities, etc.)	–230,000	
Net Income Before Taxes & Depreciation	250,000	
Taxes	–50,000	
Depreciation	–25,000	
Net Profit	175,000	BOTTOM LINE

Source: Adapted from Investopedia Inc. Search online for "Investopedia, bottom line", or follow the QR code.

number as that number determines whether the company can sustain its business for the next period. If a company's bottom line needs improvement, a company can attempt to increase their top line (by generating more sales) or they can decrease their expenditures (by cutting their cost of goods and/or operating/or other expenses). A company wishing to increase their top line generally ends up increasing their expenses as well, due to incurring greater marketing, production, personnel, or technology expenses. A company that chooses to decrease their expenditures may find themselves less productive (due to cuts in marketing, personnel, supplies) and in turn a decrease their top line. Therefore, successful companies must attempt to constantly juggle and balance their income and their expenses in order to be profitable.

While doing that strategic balancing act on the big picture of the income statement, companies must also remain nimble as they balance their cost sheets. If they cost a product too low, they will not make a sustainable profit. If they cost too high, they won't sell as many units as needed. Keeping expenses, profits, and costing at balanced is like juggling while standing on one foot and hopping in circles. You may get really good at it, then along comes someone who shakes up the room, and you have to start all over again. And that is what is happening in the fashion world today.

Now let's get to that juggling!

Key Terms

bottom line
chargebacks
discount
income statement

markdowns
profit
top line

1 Costing Basics

Costing garments is a function performed by many fashion professionals and at various times throughout a style's development. More than just calculating what a garment will cost, costing assists in fine-tuning a style specifically for a particular **target customer** or price.

The Role of Costing

Depending on the size of the company, costing is performed by many different individuals and departments. In a small company, the costing may be done by the owner or the designer. Costing is often performed by the production manager or merchandiser in a mid-sized company.

In a large company, the costing may be performed by the product or wholesale manager. Lastly, in a very large firm, there is an actual costing manager position. Smaller companies will often utilize Excel or another spreadsheet

application to calculate their costing, while in larger firms, costing is performed within their **Product Lifecycle Management** (**PLM**) software. PLM software manages the information of a style through design, development, material procurement, production and distribution process. Larger companies will use PLM or another similar software system. For this workbook, however, all costing will be explained and calculated manually. In order for a fashion professional to cost with PLM or any other software, they must first understand the numbers, how to calculate them, and the thought processes of good costing. No matter who (owner, designer, product or costing manager) is performing the costing and how (manually, Excel, or PLM) cost sheets are completed, costing garments requires outstanding analytical skills, a precise attention to detail, and an ability to negotiate. These skills are utilized during the development, production, and completion stages of each style, as at each of these times during garment-making we engage in costing. In this workbook, we will refer to these separate, but interconnected, stages in which we cost as the "costing timeline."

The Costing Timeline

Costing, when done correctly, is calculated before, during, and after a style is produced. Costing throughout the stages of production eliminates the time and money spent producing additional samples of styles that cost out too high early on in the development phase.

Many new designers cost garments after their samples have been approved. It makes more sense for them to look at their cost sheets when first evaluating a sample, as end-costing is not cost-effective if time and money went into perfecting a style, in which the cost is far greater than the target. Therefore, costing early, and costing late as well, are just as essential as costing during the production stage. The three stages of costing are: pre-production, production, and post-production costing. Let's look at all three.

Pre-Production Costing

Pre-production costing, also referred to as **sample costing**, **pre-costing**, **cost estimating**, and/or **predictive costing**, is a preliminary estimate of costs. Pre-production costing should be calculated with the first sample, as well as with each subsequent and revised sample. This costing is based on the estimated cost of fabric and trims used to create each sample, as well as on the estimate for production labor. Other cost factors (such as shipping and duties, if applicable) are estimated based on current rates. Pre-production costing is calculated with an estimated quantity, for example, how many of a style do we think we will manufacture and sell?

The advantages of pre-production costing are that as soon as you receive a sample you have a ballpark measure of what a style costs the company to make, if the style is adopted for production. This will help you evaluate the style in terms of whether or not it can work for your line. At times, pre-production costing is calculated before a sample is created, and allows a manufacturer to know whether it is worth cutting and sewing or knitting a sample at all.

Pre-production costing allows a company to determine:

* What a style will most likely cost if adopted;
* If a style can be produced at the target cost;
* And, if not, how a style can be changed so that it can lower cost by determining what is/are the largest cost factor(s) of the style, such as styling, fabric, trim, dyeing or surface treatment, labor, or transportation costs.

With this knowledge, you can proceed as is, or revise the sample so that you can reduce the quantity, complexity, or time of whichever line item is highest to bring the cost down if needed.

PRE-PRODUCTION COSTING EXAMPLE

Let's assume we are developing a style for a Victorian-themed shirt group for the fall season. In Fig. 1.1 we see a flounce-front, long-sleeve shirt with French cuffs.

Fig. 1.1 Flounce-front shirt with French cuffs.

You create a set of pages with information and detailed specifications for the styles known as a **technical package or tech pack** for short. You send the tech pack to your overseas factory, and a silk sample is returned with pre-production costing of $21.79 per piece (Table 1.1). If you are a manufacturer who has a target cost of $18–$19 (not including duty and clearance), you will know immediately upon receiving your sample that you need to make some changes to your style, or reduce your profit greatly. It is too soon to reduce your profit, as this is just a preliminary cost sheet and all costs are estimated, and there are no **indirect costs** present yet.

You will need to evaluate both the sample and the preliminary cost sheet during this pre-production costing stage. You need to decrease the costs per unit by approximately $2.80 to $3.80 in order to produce this style at your **target cost**. The target cost is the expected and maximum allowable total cost of a garment/product based on a selling price you believe your customer will pay. As your cost is too high, you need to evaluate what changes can be made to the style to hit your target cost range. We see in the preliminary cost sheet that the highest cost factor is fabric. Therefore, we must analyze ways to reduce fabric costs.

Possible Solutions for Reducing Fabric Costs
- Switch style to a lighter-weight silk crepe quality
- Reduce fabric yield by either shortening or narrowing flounce front *or* revising pattern to a standard cuff instead of French-cuff style *or* shortening blouse length
- Switch to a silk-blend fabric
- Go back to the textile mill/agent and try to negotiate a lower fabric price

The next highest cost factor is labor. Style detail and finishing changes can be made to reduce the sewing time or complexity, which would reduce labor.

Possible Solutions for Reducing Labor Costs
- Omit topstitching on collar, cuffs and/or darts
- Omit the front and back darts
- Change the hem on the front flounce to a coverstitch, instead of a rolled-hem.

These are examples of areas to cut costs early on in design development. A new cost sheet must be generated with every sample created so the designer and manufacturer can understand and know if it

Table 1.1 Preliminary cost sheet for flounce-front shirt with French cuffs

Preliminary Cost Sheet					
Date 03/2021		**Company** KRV Designs			
Style No. 1000	**Sxs No.** 200	**Season** Spring Delivery 1		**Group** Women's Victorian Tops	
Size Range XS–XL	**Sxs Size** M	**Description** Flounce Front Long Sleeve Button Down Shirt			
Fabric 16 mm Silk CDC					
Fabric	**Est. Yield**	**@Est. $/yard**	**Est. Cost**	**Total Est. Cost**	**SKETCHES**
Fabric 1: Silk CDC	1.5	$6.98	$10.47		
Lining: Interfacing	0.2	$1.99	$0.40		
Freight: Mill > Factory	1	$0.50	$0.50		
				$11.37	
Trims	**Est. Quantity**	**@Est. $/yard/gr/pc**	**Est. Cost**		
Trim 1: 18L Buttons at CF	8	$0.01	$0.08		
Trim 2: 14L Buttons at Cuff	4	$0.01	$0.05		
				$0.13	
Notions	**Est. Quantity**	**@Est. $/yard/gr/pc**	**Est. Cost**		
Notion 1: Thread	1	$0.28	$0.28		
Notion 2: Labels	1	$0.50	$0.50		
Freight: Vendor > Factory		$0.25	$0.25		
				$1.03	FRONT VIEW
Labor	**Direct**	**Contract Work**			
Cutting:	$1.55				
Sewing: China	$4.95				
Finishing: China					
Marking/Grading: China	$0.75				
				$7.25	
EST. Cost of Goods				$19.79	
Shipping	**Est. $**				
Est. Freight	$1.00				
Duty:					
Freight: Local Shipping	$1.00				
EST. SHIP				$2.00	
TOTAL COST				$21.79	
	A	**B**	**C**		
Sell Price					BACK VIEW
Net Profit					
Net Profit %					

makes sense to manufacture and sell a particular style. Another sample for the Victorian-inspired blouse would then be ordered with the revisions to bring down the costs (in order to meet the target cost of $18–$19). After sending comments to shorten front and back lengths by ¾ inch (19 mm), changing to a standard cuff, and shortening the flounce by 2 inch (51 mm)—all which reduce fabric yield—eliminating topstitching at collar and darts, and switching to a slightly lighter-weight fabric, the sketch and tech pack is revised and another sample is created (Fig. 1.2). This revised sample is within the target cost range

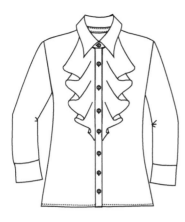

Fig. 1.2 Flounce-front shirt with standard cuffs. Note the flounce is slightly decreased in width, topstitching omitted and cuffs have been revised.

and has a pre-production costing of $18.79 per piece (not including duty and clearance) as seen in the new cost sheet (Table 1.2).

Often it takes more than two revisions to get to the target cost, but regardless of the number of cost sheets, it requires good costing skills, exercised early on and throughout the sample development process, and those skills must be applied to every line item. If yet more samples are requested for the Victorian-themed example, a preliminary cost sheet would accompany each sample. A style's cost changes with each and every change in that style's pattern, construction, fabrication, and trimming.

Once a style is approved for production, we move along to the **production costing** phase.

Production Costing

Moving along the costing timeline, we travel from the development to the production stage of each style and calculate the final production cost. Although it is a final cost, it is important to understand that costing at this stage is still an estimate; a final cost estimate. Not until production and shipping is completed, will we truly know how much it cost to produce the style.

Production costing is based on the costs of manufacturing a style once the style details are finalized and the fabric, trimming, and labor costs are known. Production costing is alternately called the **final cost**, **standard cost**, or **determined cost** and includes overheads, transportation costs, duties and customs clearance. Production costing is based on an agreed quantity of each style with the knowledge of which country the factory is located. It is essential to calculate production costing properly to ensure all materials and services the company is purchasing to produce the style will be paid for and not cut away from the desired **profit margin**. The profit margin is the percent of the selling price that is your profit.

Often a company will calculate their production costing similarly to their pre-production costing and base their production cost, or final cost, on the costs per unit. Ideally, unless only one unit is being produced, production costing should be based on the total quantity being ordered for production. Each component's cost for the entire order is divided by the total order quantity to calculate the per unit amount. That number is then inserted into the appropriate line item (fabric, trim, etc.) of the production cost sheet. Total costs for each material include excess and may include freight charges. Price negotiations are often made on the order total, as opposed to on a per-yard basis. Therefore, it is more accurate to divide the total cost of each material by the number of units being produced. This amount is the number entered on the production cost sheet.

Table 1.2 Revised cost sheet for flounce-front shirt with style and construction edits to reduce costs

Preliminary Cost Sheet					
Date 03/2021					
Style No. 1000	**Sxs No.** 200	**Season** Spring Delivery 1		**Group** Women's Victorian Tops	
Size Range XS–XL	**Sxs Size** M	**Description** Flounce Front Long Sleeve Button Down Shirt			
Fabric 14 mm Silk CDC					
Fabric	**Est. Yield**	**@Est. $/yard**	**Est. Cost**	**Total Est. Cost**	**SKETCHES**
Fabric 1: Silk CDC	1.3	$6.38	$8.29		
Lining: Interfacing	0.1	$1.99	$0.20		
Freight: Mill > Factory	1	$0.50	$0.50		
				$8.99	
Trims	**Est. Quantity**	**@Est. $/yard/gr/pc**	**Est. Cost**		
Trim 1: 18L Buttons at CF	8	$0.01	$0.08		
Trim 2: 14L Buttons at Cuff	2	$0.01	$0.02		
				$0.10	
Notions	**Est. Quantity**	**@Est. $/yard/gr/pc**	**Est. Cost**		
Notion 1: Thread	1	$0.28	$0.20		
Notion 2: Labels	1	$0.50	$0.50		
Freight: Vendor > Factory		$0.25	$0.25		
				$0.95	**FRONT VIEW**
Labor	**Direct**	**Contract Work**			
Cutting:	$1.45				
Sewing: China	$4.55				
Finishing: China					
Marking/Grading: China	$0.75				
				$6.75	
EST. Cost of Goods				$16.79	
Shipping	**Est. $**				
Est. Freight	$1.00				
Duty:					
Freight: Local Shipping	$1.00				
EST. SHIP				$2.00	
TOTAL COST				$18.79	
	A	**B**	**C**		
Sell Price					**BACK VIEW**
Net Profit					
Net Profit %					

Table 1.3 Production cost sheet for flounce-front shirt

Production Cost Sheet					
Date 03/2021		**Company** KRV Designs			
Style No. 1000	**Sxs No.** 200	**Season** Spring Delivery 1			**Group** Women's Victorian Tops
Size Range XS–XL	**Sxs Size** M	**Description** Flounce Front Long Sleeve Button Down Shirt			
Fabric 14 mm Silk CDC					
Fabric	**Yield/Style**	**Cost/Yard**	**Cost/Garment**	**Total/Garment**	**SKETCHES**
Fabric 1: Silk CDC	1.3	$6.41	$8.33		
Lining: Interfacing	0.15	$1.89	$0.28		
				$8.62	
Trims	**Yield/Style**	**Cost/Yard/ Gr/Pc**	**Cost/Garment**	**Total/Garment**	
Trim 1: 18L Buttons at CF	8	$0.01	$0.08		
Trim 2: 14L Buttons at Cuff	2	$0.01	$0.02		
				$0.10	
Notions	**Yield/Style**	**Cost/Yard/ Gr/Pc**	**Cost/Garment**	**Total/Garment**	
Notion 1: Thread	26	$8.00	$0.21		
Notion 2: Labels	1	$0.48	$0.48		
Notion 3: Hanger	1	$0.75	$0.75		
Freight: Vendor > Factory				$1.44	**FRONT VIEW**
Labor	**Country**	**Direct Labor**	**Contract Work**	**Total/Garment**	
Cutting	China	$1.45			
Sewing	China	$4.55			
Finishing		$0.40			
Marking/Grading		$0.75			
				$7.15	
Cost of Goods				$17.31	
Agent Commission %	5%	$0.87			
Freight		$0.55			
Duty %	7%	$1.21			
Clearance %	2.5%	$0.43			
Local Freight		$0.35			
LDP / DDP Cost				$20.72	
	A	**B**	**C**	**D**	**BACK VIEW**
Sell Price	$38.00	$42.00	$44.00	$46.00	
Net Profit (Sell Price less Cost)	$17.28	$21.28	$23.28	$25.28	
Net Profit % (Net Profit div by Sell)	45.48%	50.67%	52.91%	54.96%	

Looking back to the flounce-front, Victorian-inspired blouse, we see the final cost estimate calculated in the production cost sheet in Table 1.3. Now that we inserted the final costs of materials and labor, as well as duty, custom clearance, and a buying office/agent's commission (if applicable), the production cost is the amount in which we will add our desired profit margin to calculate our wholesale price. Production cost sheets often include three to four columns for calculating different profit margins and selling prices, to compare and contrast scenarios where you are closer to a desired profit versus a desired selling price.

Each line item will be further discussed in Chapter 2, but it is essential to know why production costing is important and how it differs from the other two times in which garment styles are costed. Production costing is the most strategic of the costing stages. Accuracy is essential at this stage as the **wholesale price** and, in turn, the **suggested retail price (SRP)** are finalized at this stage. The wholesale price is the cost of a product sold by a wholesaler to a retailer for resale, and the SRP is the price at which a manufacturer/wholesaler recommends that retailers sell their product. The SRP is also known as the **manufacturer's suggested retail price (MSRP)**, **recommended retail price**, or **list price**. Both the wholesale and suggested retail prices are based on the profit margin each company desires to earn. Inadvertently omitting a cost on this cost sheet is a loss and decreases the bottom line. We will not know if the production cost was exact until the next stage of the timeline: post-production costing.

Post-Production Costing

Post-production costing is the evaluation and determination of how well we have succeeded, or not, in the production costing process. Post-production costing is also referred to as **actual cost**, and it displays the actual production costs after a style is produced, shipped, and sold. At this costing stage we look at how much we spent per garment to make and deliver the style. Also, if any discounts or chargebacks were allowed, or rush freight fees paid, these figures will be reflected on a post-production cost sheet.

Once calculated, the post-production cost sheet is compared to the production cost sheet in order to assess how the costs were estimated for each style. The information gained is used for future style costing. Only after all expenses are paid and discounts given can actual cost be calculated. We then evaluate the actual cost line-by-line against the production cost estimate to determine where, in terms of materials, production, freight, and markup, we need to improve our performance—in terms of sourcing, negotiation, production, and cost calculations for the future. Additionally, and importantly, we look to post-production costing to see if we have met our profit margin. We need to evaluate if we have earned a sustainable profit.

Post-production costing is performed after the season is complete, and while you are in the midst of pre-production costing for one season and production costing for another. So good costing managers are skilled at juggling cost sheets for many different deliveries of many different styles often made in an array of factories, and possibly countries, at the same time. Costing, like fashion, is an art!

Costing Terms and Vocab

Once you are aware of the timeline when fashion styles are cost, it is important to know the basic terminology often heard regarding cost when sourcing materials or a production facility for a style.

When selecting fabrics, buttons, hang tags, and so forth, a supplier will quote a price per yard/per gross/per mil/etc. When sourcing garments, a factory will advise a price based on the quantity estimate you provide. For domestic goods, generally the price does

not include shipping to you. You will need to research and add the cost of freight to your cost sheet for all components and finished product.

The materials and labor together are known as the **Cost of Goods Sold** (**COGS**). The COGS is the costs to produce the item you'll be selling. When you source garment or accessory factories to sew or knit your production, there is vocabulary to know—regarding costing—that is generally stated in the form of abbreviations. These abbreviations include what particular garment-production services and activities are included in the quoted factory price. It is imperative to understand these as they affect your cost sheet calculations. Factories will advise production prices in several different ways; each varies on a factory's responsibilities:

- **CM** (Cut and Make): This is a garment-production term meaning the cost for the garments/items to be cut and sewn. This is a labor-only price and does not include pattern making, materials, tagging, packing, shipping or taxes. The responsibility of the factory is only to make the goods.
- **CMT** (Cut, Make, and Trim): This is a garment-production term and refers to the cost for the garments/items to be cut, sewn, trimmed, tagged/labeled, inspected, and packed. This price generally does not include patternmaking and materials (but at times does) nor shipping or taxes.
- **CMTP** (Cut, Make, Trim and Pack): This is a garment-production term that includes the cost for the garments/items to be cut, sewn, trimmed, tagged/labeled, inspected, and packed (basically the same as CMT, although some CMTP factories perform full package production as well, and therefore this can be a confusing term).
- **FPP** (Full Package Production): This is a garment-production term that means it is the cost for the garments/items to be cut, sewn, trimmed, tagged/labeled, inspected, and packed, and includes patternmaking, sampling, and purchasing of raw materials. This price does not include shipping or taxes.

As stated earlier, costing is a precise, detail-oriented skill which involves analyzing every line item. Each and every decision made regarding a garment affects that garment's cost, as does all material, pattern, and construction changes along the way. Therefore, cost sheets are in a constant state of revision. Additionally, every quote received from a supplier of fabric, trims, findings, sewing, or finishing services may or may not be the full cost to purchase and receive that material or service. So, there is always the possibility that there is an additional cost that is missed on a cost sheet if you are not paying close attention to each item. Costing is the area that is the most important to watch carefully, as a mistake in costing can cost the company a great deal, even if the style is a best seller.

Summary

Basic costing helps design the line and specify a target customer. It is implemented by various persons within the company, that is, owner, merchandiser, costing manager, and depending on company size a variety of options is at their disposal: for example, manually, using Excel, or PLM. Basic costing is performed throughout the stages of development, production, and order completion/distribution.

Costing throughout the production process reduces time and money spent. Pre-production costing is a preliminary estimate of costs and is calculated based on the first sample estimates; fabric, trims, labor, shipping, duties. Estimated quantities manufactured and sold must also be taken into account. This helps determine if a product should be adopted for production or needs to be adjusted. At times, this is even done before a sample is created.

Next, production costing, which is still an estimate is based on manufacturing a style once the fabric, trim, and labor are known. This should include overheads such as transportation costs, duties, and customs clearance. The quantity produced and the country the factory is located are determined. All materials and services the company is purchasing must be accounted for in order to not cut away at the profit margin. The profit margin is the percent of the selling price that is your profit. Production costing is the most strategic of the costing stages.

Finally, post-production costing is an evaluation of the actual cost to produce, ship, and sell the style. Discounts, chargebacks, rush freight fees are paid and compared to production cost sheet. This is then used for future style costing and analyzed line by line.

Chapter Review and Discussion

1. If you were going to place an ad on a job search site for a costing manager, what would be the duties and skill set you would include in the posting?
2. What are the three stages that a product is costed? How does each costing phase differ?
3. Why are the line items on a cost sheet constantly changing? What factors do you think might make the figures on the line items change?
4. List the differences among the four garment-production price-quotation terms: CM, CMT, CMTP, and FPP.
5. Why do you think many fashion professionals choose to negotiate the CMT price of a garment?
6. Why is it important to cost early and often in the development of a product or garment style?

Activities and Exercises

1. You are working on a new style knit style for your collection to be manufactured in America. This new style is a striped, long-sleeve, knit top for a future season. This knit top is crew neck with a rib around the neckline, has an all-over, horizontal, yarn-dye stripe fabric of 100 percent cotton. In addition, the cuffs and bottom sweep opening are ribbed and utilizing a single-needle topstitch to attach the cuffs and bottom hem opening to the body. After planning on producing a particular garment and after costing it out, you are not making a healthy margin on this garment. What are some of the different elements or changes you can implement to bring down the cost and make a better margin?

2. Find and research a high-end fashion designer brand's style. This could be a pair of trousers, a shirt, or a jacket. Be sure to look at the country of origin (**COO**), the fiber content, any major construction details, the quality of fabric, stitching, and any trims/materials used. From there, act as a product development (**PD**) manager and "adapt" this style for your mass market brand. What changes would you employ and incorporate into this style to create a brand new, lower price point style?

Key Terms

actual cost

CM (cut and make)

CMT (cut, make, trim, and pack)

COGS (cost of goods)

COO (country of origin)

cost estimating

determined cost

final cost

FPP (full package production)

indirect costs

list price

MSRP (manufacturer's suggested retail price)

PLM (product lifecycle management)

post-production costing

pre-costing

pre-production costing

predictive costing

production costing

profit margin

sample costing

SRP (suggested retail price)

standard cost

target cost

target customer

technical package

wholesale price

2 Traditional Apparel Costing

Introduction

Costing garments is a function performed by many fashion professionals and at various times throughout the development of a style. More than just calculating what a garment will cost, costing assists in fine-tuning a style specifically for a particular target customer or price.

Traditional costing with long-established cost sheets is the way that many fashion companies operate, especially smaller, local, and/or start-up fashion businesses. Traditional costing includes the basics: the costs of materials plus labor, plus profit.

The **direct cost** factors, materials and labor, are tallied, and the desired markup is added. Traditional costing is calculated on a basic cost sheet (see Table 2.1).

The materials include fabric, lining, trim, notions, and any other tangible raw items that are used to create a particular style. Labor includes pattern making, cutting, sewing, tagging, packing, and any other direct labor that goes into making a particular style. These

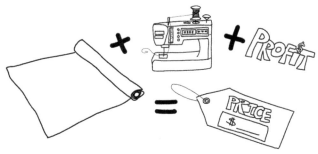

two columns of factors are added to obtain the **first cost (FC)**. Let's look closer at first cost.

First Cost

The FC, also referred to as direct cost, is straightforward. It is the sum of the costs of the fabric, lining, trims, notions, pattern, and all required labor.

> **Materials and Labor = First Cost**

Assuming you have a first sample, the FC is the materials and production work that went into manufacturing the sample. If you do not have a first sample, you can estimate the FC by looking at a similar past style's information, in terms of how much fabric and trims were consumed, as well as labor times and rates. When referring to a past style, it is best to use the post-production cost sheet for reference, as that is the most accurate.

Table 2.1 Step 1—Add front and back flat sketches

Preliminary Basic Cost Sheet					
Date		**Company**			
Style No.	**Sxs No.**	**Season**		**Group**	
Size Range	**Sxs Size**	**Description**			
Fabric					
Fabric	**Est. Yield**	**@Est. $/yard**	**Est. Cost**	**Total Est. Cost**	**SKETCHES**
Fabric 1:					
Fabric 2:					
Freight:					
				$0.00	
Trims	**Est. Quantity**	**@Est. $/ yard/gr/pc**	**Est. Cost**		
Trim 1:					
Trim 2:					
Trim 3:					
Freight:					
				$0.00	
Notions	**Est. Quantity**	**@Est. $/ yard/gr/pc**	**Est. Cost**		
Notion 1:					
Notion 2:					
Freight:					
				$0.00	
Labor	**Direct**	**Contract Work**			**FRONT VIEW**
Cutting:					
Sewing:					
Finishing:					
Marking/Grading:					
				$0.00	
EST. First Cost of Goods				$0.00	
		Markup Goal %	**100%–MU%**	**Markup $**	
Selling Price					
					BACK VIEW

Let's look at the FC components separately. Materials, which include fabric and trim, are generally the greater portion of FC.

Fabric Cost

Fabric is largely the greatest factor on a cost sheet, and in most cases, fabric has a higher cost than all other materials and labor in producing a garment. All fabric involved in creating a style must go on the cost sheet. This includes lining fabric and fabric used as trim. Each fabric is its own line item on the cost sheet. At each line item you input the **fabric yield** or **fabric consumption**—this is the amount of fabric required (per yard or meter) to make one style. The price for each fabric is also noted on the cost sheet. The fabric cost is entered with the unit of measurement it is sold in: that is, cost/per yard or cost/per meter. The amount of each fabric per style is then multiplied by the fabric cost to determine the cost of each fabric for each garment.

Fabric	Yield/Style	Cost/Unit	Cost/Garment
Fabric 1: 100% cotton 14 oz. denim	2 yards or 1.85 meters	$6.99/yard or $7.57/meter	$13.98
Fabric 2: 100% cotton plain-weave pocketing	0.125 yards or 0.13 meters	$1.40/yard or $1.52/meter	$0.18
Total Fabric			$14.16

Cost Sheet 3: Calculating Materials per style/per order

On a cost sheet, when styles are created from more than one fabric, the fabrication is listed from the fabric that is used most first to the fabric that is used the least. If shipping is not included in the fabric prices, which generally it is not, then freight must be added to the fabric total.

Fabric	Yield/Style	Cost/Unit	Cost/Garment
Fabric 1: 100% cotton 14 oz. denim	2 yards or 1.85 meters	$6.99/yard or $7.57/meter	$13.98
Fabric 2: 100% cotton plain-weave pocketing	0.125 yards or 0.13 meters	$1.40/yard or $1.52/meter	$0.18
Total Fabric			$14.16
Shipping (mill to factory)	$0.50		$14.66

Cost Sheet 3: Calculating Materials per style/per order

Also, fabric can be notated as exterior-fabric, shell-fabric, or body-fabric (which is the outside or main fabric) and then the lining (which is the interior fabric). Other fabric that is listed includes fabric used as small body parts or trims such as when different fabrics are used for collars, cuffs, inside plackets or waistbands, pocket bag lining, fabric bindings, pipings or tapes, and those fabrics are also included on the cost sheet. When the exterior- or body-fabric is used as the lining or for the trims (i.e., to cover buttons or create piping), then it is referred to as **self-fabric.** Self-fabric means that fabrication used is the same fabric that is used for the exterior or body of the garment.

When determining fabric cost, you must calculate the fabric consumption by considering all of the factors that affect how much fabric a particular style will take. Factors that must be considered include the fabric width, fabric layout/print/direction, sample size, the size range and wastage. Here is an explanation of each of these factors:

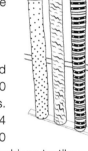

FABRIC WIDTH

Another key element to consider is fabric width, because not all fabric is woven or knitted in the same width. Standard fabric widths are 44/45 inches (1,100/1,100 mm) or 58/60 inches (1,500/1,500 mm). However, fabric also comes in many narrower and wider widths. Fabric widths include 35–36 inches (890–910 mm), 38–39 inches (950–990 mm), 52–54 inches (1,300–1,400 mm), 72 inches (1,800 mm), 84 inches (2100 mm), 96 inches (2,400 mm), 108 inches (2,700 mm), and up to 118–120 inches (3,000–3,000 mm) for home fashions textiles.

FC fabric consumption is based on the amount of fabric needed to make one garment, which varies depending on the width of the fabric (see Chart 2.1).

Chart 2.1 Fabric Consumption Chart

STYLESIZE	FABRIC WIDTH	YIELD (in YARDS)	YIELD (in METERS)
Men's button-front shirt 40" Chest X 15" Neck	35–36"	2	1.8288
	44–45"	1.75	1.6002
	50–52"	1.5	1.3716
	58–60"	1.25	1.143
	70–72"	1	0.9144
Adult short-sleeve tee M	35–36"	1.50	1.3716
	44–45"	1.25	1.143
	50–52"	1	0.9144
	58–60"	0.75	0.68
	70–72"	0.5	0.45

Men's jeans 32" X 32"	35–36"	2	1.8
	44–45"	1.75	1.6
	50–52"	1.5	1.37
	58–60"	1.25	1.14
	70–72"	1	0.9
Women's tank top M	35–36"	1	0.9
	44–45"	0.875	0.8
	50–52"	0.75	0.7
	58–60"	0.625	0.6
	70–72"	0.5	0.45
Women's skirt w/ flounce 8	35–36"	1	0.9
	44–45"	0.875	0.8
	50–52"	0.75	0.7
	58–60"	0.625	0.6
	70–72"	0.5	0.45
Women's dress 8	35–36"	2	1.8
	44–45"	1.75	1.6
	50–52"	1.5	1.37
	58–60"	1.375	1.3
	70–72"	1.25	1.15

Highlighted Hint: Approximate fabric yields for various styles

FABRIC LAYOUT, PRINT, AND DIRECTION

An important factor when determining how much fabric is needed is if a fabric has a print or pattern. Typically, prints and patterns require a greater fabric yield per style. Whether a fabric has a repeat print, one-way print, two-way print, selvedge border design, or is a stripe or plaid are all factors in determining fabric consumption. If the design or pattern must match at center front, side seams, and pockets, then this increases the fabric yield.

The border print fabric pattern is placed differently so the border print appears at the bottom hem, sleeve, and top of pocket. As you can imagine, each fabric is different and must be analyzed based on the fabric characteristics. The amount of fabric required to make one garment in based on whether the fabric is or pattern. The more fabric needed, for instance, for a fabric with a pattern, the higher the fabric cost/per style.

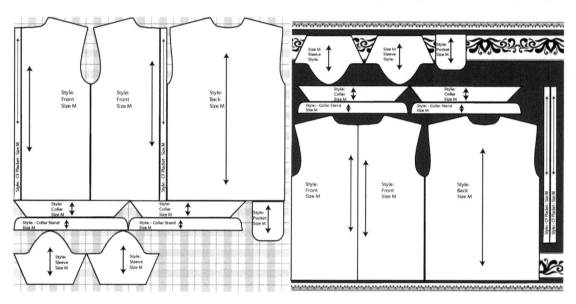

Fig. 2.1 Pattern and Print Direction. The plaid print above has been designed using resources from Freepik.com.

Here are two single-size pattern layouts. The gingham plaid print (on the left) shows the side seams placed side by side. This layout allows the stripes of the plaid to line up perfectly at the seams and along center front, maintaining a quality stripe aesthetic. The border print (on the right) shows the pattern pieces placed strategically along the filigree-border print. This layout allows the print borders to be engineered so the print will go across the edges of the pocket, sleeve hems, and along the shirt bottom.

SAMPLE SIZE

Fabric consumption on a traditional cost sheet is based on the sample size in which the samples are being made. Samples are used for fitting, style revision, selling, and approval. Sample sizes are generally created with a 40 inch (1,000 mm) chest and 32 inch (800 mm) waist for men's wear, in a size 8 or 10 for womenswear, a size 18 or 20 for women's, a size 5 or 7 for junior women's, and in a size 7 or 8 for girl's or boy's wear. The same sample size will be used throughout the line to ensure consistency in both size and cost.

It is worth noting the average women's size in the United States is currently a size 16. As inclusive-size clothing increases in demand, more brands are increasing their offerings up to size 22. One problem that companies face while developing a product line is trying to accommodate customers from a size 2 to a size

22 with the same designs. **Grading,** adjusting the sample size to create the pattern for smaller and larger sizes, is more difficult with a wider size range. It is advised to design specifically for larger body types.

SIZE RANGE

Deciding the size range you plan to produce is instrumental for costing and determining target price, as this affects fabric consumption and cost—especially if you are planning to produce in larger sizes. Fabric yields can be first calculated on your sample size. However, if you plan on producing greater quantities of your larger sizes, the final outcome is greatly affected. If you are producing a wide range of sizes, you should average the estimated quantities of each size and plan your fabric consumption on the median size—which is often not the sample size. If you plan to do a wide range of sizes, you may consider breaking into petite, regular, and plus, giving each a sample size and in return costing each size range separately. This will also help with fitting garments down the road. The sample size should be the middle size. For example, if the line's size range is sizes 2–14, then a size 8 would be the sample size. The average American woman is now a size 16 or 18. It is worth noting if larger sizes are to be produced to split the size range into two, for example, size 2–12 and size 14–22. This would make the smaller size range sample size 8 and the large size range sample size an 18.

SIZE SCALE

After deciding the size range, next, size scale is to be determined. The size scale is the ratio used during manufacturing to produce different quantities based on size. For example, if a designer decides to produce size small, medium, large, and extra large, they may want to produce more size medium and large, and less small and extra large. In order to communicate this to the manufacturer, a size scale is given.

Size	Small	Medium	Large	Extra Large
Ratio	1	2	2	1

This chart shows that for every one small and one extra large cut and sewn, there will be two medium and large cut and sewn. This also impacts the yield. For example, if a designer decides to do an even-size scale—small, medium, large, extra large in a 2-2-2-2 ratio—the fabric yield may be more or less, but other factors such as fabric width and fabric type must be taken into account.

WASTAGE

Fabric waste is inevitable and must be considered. Wastage occurs from the irregular fabric shapes that are left between pattern pieces after cutting (as seen by all the grey areas in Image), or from irregularities in the yardage, cutting or sewing errors, dirt, and water or mildew damage that possibly resulted during transport or storage. Generally, 10–15 percent of fabric is wasted, due to any of these given reasons. Therefore, a minimum of 10 percent excess fabric must be ordered—and included on your cost sheet—to accommodate the many possible ways that fabric is wasted.

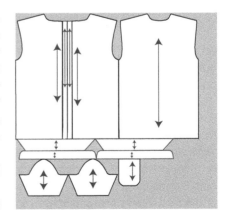

When selecting and purchasing fabric for design and production, all of the aforementioned need to be considered. Many of these factors are also taken into account when sourcing trims, notions, and findings.

Trim Cost

Trims, findings, notions, and structural components are included in the materials that go into the FC. Trims are decorative and they include embroidery, patches, and ribbon. Notions and findings are functional and include zippers, hook-and-eyes, collar stays, labels, and snaps. They can also provide structure and shape to a garment, such as shoulder pads, interfacing and boning. Buttons are technically a finding since they serve a function and are most often referred to as a trim. All trims, findings/notions, and structure pieces, plus hangtags and poly bags, affect garment cost.

Each trim or finding selected for a style is also an item on the cost sheet. The amount/quantity of trim needed to make each style, as well as the cost of each trim, is noted and multiplied, as is calculated with fabric cost. The trim cost, if it is a linear trim, such as ribbon, ric-rac, or piping, is entered with the linear unit of measurement in which it is sold: that is, cost/per yard or cost/per meter. The trim cost if it is a loose item, such as buttons, beads, or snaps, is entered with the quantity in pieces in which it is sold: that is, cost/per gross or cost/per mille. A gross is 144 pieces and a mille is 1,000 pieces.

The amount of each trim or finding per style is then multiplied by the cost to determine the cost of each fabric for each garment.

Trim	Yield or Qty/Style	Cost/Unit	Cost/Garment
Trim 1: 20 mm antique silver metal shank	1 piece	$0.25/piece	$0.25
Trim 2: 9 mm antique silver metal rivets	10 pieces	$.10/piece	$1.00
Trim 3: Metal zipper	1	$0.25/piece	$0.25
Total Trim			$1.50
Shipping (trim vendor to factory)	$0.25		$1.75

BOM: Filled in sample of this key part of every tech pack

An additional item in the case of trims, specifically in the case of buttons, is the extra button. If an extra button is specified to be included with a style, the additional button must be added to the included in the quantity on the cost sheet.

Thread is a component that is in every sewn garment. It is not a trim, as it holds the seams together, but stitch lines can be used as trim, such as double- or triple-needle seam finishes. Thread is a cost factor that varies greatly depending on the complexity of the garment styling and on the ways each seam is stitched and finished. The more labor intensive and the larger or more complex the garment is, the more thread it will consume. Here are a few common garment styles and their average thread consumption, based on Coats, one of the best-selling thread company's website (Coats 2014). Search online for "Coats threads", or follow the QR code here to find more on the Coats website.

Style (Adult size medium, unless noted)	Avg Thread Consumed (in yards/meters)	Plus 10% Wastage	Total Thread Yield Including Wastage
Blouse	103 yd / 95 m	10 yd / 10 m	113 yd / 105 m
Bra	46 yd / 43 m	5 yd / 4 m	51 yd / 47 m
Dress (girls)	92 yd / 85 m	10 yd / 9 m	102 yd / 94 m
Dress (ladies)	200 yd / 185 m	20 yd / 19 m	220 yd / 204 m
Jeans (mens)	216 yd / 200 m	22 yd / 20 m	238 yd / 220 m
Tank top	52 yd / 48 m	5 yd / 4 m	57 yd / 52 m
Shirt (boys)	78 yd / 75 m	8 yd / 8 m	86 yd / 83 m
Shirt (mens)	125 yd / 115 m	13 yd / 12 m	138 yd / 127 m
Suit (mens)	494 yd / 460 m	49 yd / 46 m	543 yd / 506 m
T-shirt	103 yd / 95 m	10 yd / 10 m	113 yd / 105 m

Highlighted Hint: Estimated thread consumption for various styles

Please know that thread consumption varies greatly depending on whether you are sewing with a single, double, or triple needle; lockstitch; or coverstich. The aforementioned examples are of average thread consumption per style. Adding decorative topstitching or a serged hem, as opposed to a straight hem, would increase the thread consumption. Taking the coverstitch seam allowances away would decrease thread consumption.

Just as waste, sadly but inevitably, occurs and must be considered with fabric. This too is the case with findings and trims. Wastage in these cases often occur simply from loss due to the small size of many buttons, beads and so forth. Or in the case of linear trims (those purchased by the yard/meter, such as ribbon or piping), waste is caused by irregularities, dirt, or water/mildew damage from transport or storage. Generally, 10 percent of trims and notions are wasted or unusable, and therefore 10 percent should be added to the cost sheet.

Once you have your fabric and trim quantities needed to produce a style, you enter all fabric and trims onto the cost sheet. Now, let's move onto labor, the next factor in the FC.

Direct Labor Costs

All direct labor activities must be included on the cost sheet. Direct labor includes pattern making, marker making, cutting, sewing, pressing, labeling, and so forth. Additionally, if a style requires any piece work, such as hand-beading, that is also included as direct labor.

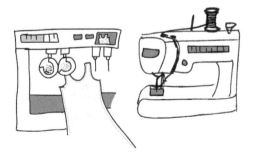

Generally, each labor activity is separately calculated to determine each labor activity's cost. Labor costs are computed by multiplying the time needed to perform a particular step in minutes or hours by the hourly or daily rate a worker is paid. Let's look at each labor activity separately.

Table 2.2 Step 2—Add in style information at the top of the sheet along with material pricing and quantities

CREATING A COST SHEET

Start by filling out the Cost Sheet heading for all the important necessary information such as dates and categories

Then, list each FABRIC needed to create the garment along with the quantities and pricing

Multiply the amount of yards by the given price per yard and add up to get your TOTAL FABRIC COST

Follow the same steps as above for all your TRIM and NOTIONS

Preliminary Basic Cost Sheet					
Date 03/10/2021		**Company** KRV Designs			
Style No. 1111	**Sxs No.** 210	**Season** Spring Delivery 1		**Group** Men's Denim Bottoms	
Size Range 28-36	**Sxs Size** 32	**Description** 5-Pocket Denim Jean Relaxed Fit Jean			
Fabric 14 Oz 100% Cotton Denim - 60"					
Fabric	Est. Yield	@Est. $/yard	Est. Cost	Total Est. Cost	**SKETCHES**
Fabric 1: 14 oz Denim	2	$ 6.99	$13.98		
Fabric 2: Plainweave	0.125	$1.40	$0.18		
Freight: Mill > Factory	1	$0.50	$0.50		
				$14.66	
Trims	Est. Quantity	@Est. $/yard/gr/pc	Est. Cost		
Trim 1: 20 mm Antique Silver Metal Shank	1	$0.25	$0.25		
Trim 2: 9 mm Antique Silver Metal Rivets	10	$0.10	$1.00		
Trim 3: Metal Zipper	1	$0.25	$0.25		
Freight: Vendor > Factory	1	$0.25	$0.25		
				$1.75	
Notions	Est. Quantity	@Est. $/yard/gr/pc	Est. Cost		
Notion 1: Thread	1	$1.00	$1.00		
Notion 2: Logo Back Patch	1	$0.50	$0.50		
Freight: Vendor > Factory	1	$0.25	$0.25		
				$1.75	**FRONT VIEW**
Labor	**Direct**	Contract Work			
Cutting:					
Sewing:					
Finishing:					
Marking/Grading:					
				$0.00	
EST. First Cost of Goods					
		Markup Goal %	100%– MU%	Markup $	
Selling Price					
					BACK VIEW

PATTERN MAKING

Pattern making is the creation of a **sloper**: a basic paper pattern which when cut and sewn will cover a three-dimensional surface. Creating a pattern can be done by using measurements to draft on paper, fabric to drape over a dress form, and/or inputting measurements into computer pattern-making software. Also known as a garment engineer, a pattern maker affects the cost of

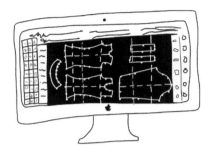

a garment greatly by the means the pattern is produced. A pattern maker can charge upwards of $300 dollars for an initial pattern, not including corrections. This and other pattern-making charges, fittings, adjustments, and production patterns, must be taken into account throughout the costing process. Producing a digital pattern can cut the time it takes a pattern maker to create a pattern, but digital pattern-making equipment (plotters) are expensive, and take great knowledge and experience.

GRADING

Once the production pattern is finalized, grading and marking begins. Grading a garment begins by deciding how large or small the pattern will change at each pattern point to create additional sizes. For example, sample size medium will have a 1 inch (25 mm) increase at the chest and sweep to create size large, but a 1 inch (25 mm) decrease to create the small size. Each **point of measure** must be

Mmt:	2	4	6	8	10	12	14	16
Bust	−1	−1	−1	36	+1½	+1½	+1½	+1½
Waist	−1	−1	−1	28	+1½	+1½	+1½	+1½
Hi-Hip	−1	−1	−1	35	+1½	+1½	+1½	+1½
Lo-Hip	−1	−1	−1	38	+1½	+1½	+1½	+1½
Armhole	−½	−½	−½	16	+¾	+¾	+¾	+¾
Cross Back	−¼	−¼	−¼	14	+⅜	+⅜	+⅜	+⅜
Thigh	−¾	−¾	−¾	22½	+1	+1	+1	+1

WOMEN'S GRADING – MISSY – KRV+Co.

taken into account. Grading can be done manually but to be done precisely and efficiently, it should be done using a plotter. A professional grader will request the final production pattern and the specification sheet with grade rules, as well as the breakdown of sizes to be marked to create the final marker. The cost of grading and creating a marker can cost $15–$20 each if done in the United States. When working with a factory overseas, this cost is usually included in the price of the factory quote.

MARKER MAKING

Marker making is conducted once the pattern and fabric are finalized. Taking into account the fabric width and the sizes you plan to produce, a puzzle-like blue print is created from the traced pattern pieces. Good markers will produce a low fabric yield with minimal wastage. Once a pattern is digitized and the graded sizes are created, it is easy to print different marker widths and different breakdowns using pattern-making software. As mentioned previously in size scale, a marker can have one of each size, but perhaps it would make more sense producing more medium and large sizes than small and x-large sizes. Fig. 2.2 shows a digital marker with sizes XS–S–M–L pants, courtesy of Top Notch Pattern Inc.

CUTTING

Cutting is the process of having all pattern pieces required to create a style cut from the fabric. The fabric is first spread on a cutting table. It can be spread across the cutting table in one single layer; this is known as single-ply and is laid this way when producing only one of a style at a time. Most often fabric is laid in multiple layers; this is known as multi-ply, and allows for multiple pieces to be cut simultaneously. Fabric may be cut manually with a fabric scissor, semiautomatically with handheld cutting machines, or digitally with a fully automatic digital cutting system.

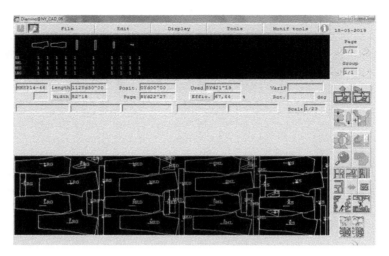

Fig. 2.2 Digital marker with sizes XS–S–M–L pants, courtesy of Top Notch Pattern Inc.

In an email conversation with Daniella Ambrogi, VP of Marketing at Lectra, Daniella wrote:

Depending on the weight of each fabric, Lectra's digital cutting systems can cut through up to 100 layers of fabric (100-ply), for a lingerie-weight fabric, for instance. Automated digital cutting machines can cut up to 9 centimeters of fabric at one time, allowing multiple patterns pieces to be cut at once, accurately and at an extremely high-speed. Lectra's Cutting Room 4.0 platform can cut up to 130 meters of single-ply fabric per minute, detect and cut around fabric flaws, and even optimize the best way to cut various fabric patterns, saving marker-making time when matching stripes, or borders. Therefore, for a designer or brand, a factory utilizing fully-automated digital cutting is the most cost- and time-efficient option of the three; as well automated cutting reduces fabric waste.

Generally, cutting cost is calculated by multiplying the cutting time by the cutter's wages, then dividing by the number of units being cut at one time times the number of fabric plies. Therefore, the cutting method (manual or digital), the number of plies being cut at one time, the number of pattern pieces, the number of color combinations, and whether the cut pieces need to be bundled (tied together) and labeled can all affect the cutting cost.

SEWING

Sewing is the one garment-making activity that, at least for the time being, still largely requires people to either perform some amount of stitching by hand or to program and operate the machines. A person or group of persons in a production line must sew the seams and assemble the garments. Grading, marking, spreading, and cutting can be performed automatically, and automation is in the innovation stage for sewing, but there are still sewing machines operators at every factory—loads of them.

Factory-sewing costs are calculated by determining the time it takes to sew each detail and seam. Due to the fact that entire garments are most often not sewn by one person, the sewing labor is determined by figuring out the length of time it takes to complete all the many sewing steps (or actions) needed to sew a particular style. All sewing actions are timed and added together to get the total sewing time and cost. Each individual sewing detail or seam is timed to determine that activity's **standard allowed minutes** (**SAMs**).

In an overseas factory, one serged side-seam or double-needle hem stitched is each equivalent to approximately 0.5 SAMs. That translates to each of those actions taking 30 seconds each for a sewer to perform. One attached neck band takes 1.0 SAMs. Sewers are timed performing the same sewing action multiple times to determine the SAM for a particular activity, then 20 percent additional time is added to the time of each step to compensate for individual machine or personal allowances, as well as 10 percent is added for moving the finished piece to the next step. Therefore, a total of 30 percent is added to the total time to calculate the SAM of a style.

A basic T-shirt may be timed and averaged for a total of 4.25 minutes in a large Chinese factory to sew. Thirty percent is added to that time to arrive at the SAM for that style (20 percent for machine and personal allowance and 10 percent for moving or bundling). It is then calculated that the total basic T-shirt is 5.5 SAMs (five-and-one-half minutes) to complete the sewing of that one shirt. Then 5.5 would be multiplied by the average wage (in minutes) of a sewer. In China, the average garment worker makes $270/month (Lu 2018) that equates to $12.85/day. When a T-shirt takes 5.5 SAMs to sew, that means the Chinese sewer makes that shirt $0.15/each (Lu 2018). Labor is unfortunately not a large cost factor on many lines. Search online for "Sheng Lu fashion, FASH455", or follow the QR code for further details.

The more labor-intensive styles, of course, are the more complex styles, and those require more time to sew, and have higher SAMs and related labor costs. Each sewn buttonhole, placket, pin tuck, dart, and detail requires more sewing time and, in turn, increases the labor cost of an item.

SAMs vary greatly depending on fabric/finding/trim types, stitches per inch, factory line layout, and factory or country culture. Search online for "Online Clothing Study, Basic Garment Products, Sarkar", or follow the QR code for further details on SAMs.

Here are a few common garment styles and the average SAM for each style (Sarkar 2011, Talekar 2014, Apparel Costing 2017).

Style (Adult size medLium, unless noted)	Avg SAMs
Blouse	18.0
Bra	18.0
Jeans	13.0
Shirt (mens dress)	21.5
Shirt (mens polo)	13.75
Suit jacket (mens)	101.0
Suit pants (mens)	35.0
T-shirt	5.5

PIECE WORK: TRIMMING AND EMBELLISHMENT

As every sewing step takes time and adds to the labor cost, so does trimming and embellishment. Trimming and embellishment is decorative and can include screen printing a placement design on the front of a tee, the beading on a collar, adding rhinestones to yoke, or pick-stitching a lapel. As in sewing, the time to add the design detail is timed and multiplied by the piece worker daily rate. Piecework such as this, can often be very costly, as other than the rate to add the embellishment, often the garment that will be trimmed are all cut and bundled, and then taken to another area of a factory, or to another factory altogether to be embellished. They are then returned to the general sewing assembly area, so there is generally a logistics cost included with the labor.

Table 2.3 Step 3—Add up total fabric, trim, and notion costs to prepare for adding total labor costs

CREATING A COST SHEET

Now you have added in your Total Fabric, Total Trim and Total Notions costs

➤ Total Fabric

➤ Total Trim

➤ Total Notions

From here, add in the Total LABOR for Cutting, Sewing, Finishing and Marking/ Grading costs for the country in which you choose to manufacture your goods

Preliminary Basic Cost Sheet					
Date 03/10/2021		**Company** KRV Designs			
					Group Men's Denim Bottoms
Style No. 1111	**Sxs No.** 210	**Season** Spring Delivery 1			
Size Range 28-36	**Sxs Size** 32	**Description** 5-Pocket Denim Jean Relaxed Fit Jean			
Fabric 14 Oz 100% Cotton Denim - 60"					
Fabric	Est. Yield	@Est. $/yard	Est. Cost	Total Est. Cost	**SKETCHES**
Fabric 1: 14 oz Denim	2	$6.99	$13.98		
Fabric 2: Plainweave	0.125	$1.40	$0.18		
Freight: Mill > Factory	1	$0.50	$0.50		
				$14.66	
Trims	Est. Quantity	@Est. $/ yard/gr/pc	Est. Cost		
Trim 1: 20 mm Antique Silver Metal Shank	1	$0.25	$0.25		
Trim 2: 9 mm Antique Silver Metal Rivets	10	$0.10	$1.00		
Trim 3: Metal Zipper	1	$0.25	$0.25		
Freight: Vendor > Factory	1	$0.25	$0.25		
				$1.75	
Notions	Est. Quantity	@Est. $/ yard/gr/pc	Est. Cost		
Notion 1: Thread	1	$1.00	$1.00		
Notion 2: Logo Back Patch	1	$0.50	$0.50		
Freight: Vendor > Factory	1	$0.25	$0.25		
				$1.75	**FRONT VIEW**
Labor	**Direct**	**Contract Work**			
Cutting: China	$1.45				
Sewing: China	$4.55				
Finishing: China	$0.75				
Marking/ Grading: China	$0.75				
				$7.50	
EST. First Cost of Goods					
		Markup Goal %	100% −MU%	Markup $	
Selling Price					
					BACK VIEW

Table 2.4 Step 4—Add in the total labor costs. From there, add up the total materials and labor to arrive at first cost

CREATING A COST SHEET

At this point, you must now add up the Total Fabric Cost
+
Total Trim Cost
+
Total Notions Cost
+
Total Labor Cost

Adding these together bring you to your FIRST COST OF GOODS

Total First Cost →

Date 03/10/2021		Company KRV Designs			
					Group Men's Denim Bottoms
Style No. 1111	**Sxs No.** 210	**Season** Spring Delivery 1			
Size Range 28-36	**Sxs Size** 32	**Description** 5-Pocket Denim Jean Relaxed Fit Jean			
Fabric 14 Oz 100% Cotton Denim - 60"					
Fabric	Est. Yield	@Est. $/yard	Est. Cost	Total Est. Cost	**SKETCHES**
Fabric 1: 14 oz Denim	2	$6.99	$13.98		
Fabric 2: Plainweave	0.125	$1.40	$0.18		
Freight: Mill > Factory	1	$0.50	$0.50		
				$14.66	
Trims	Est. Quantity	@Est. $/yard/gr/pc	Est. Cost		
Trim 1: 20 mm Antique Silver Metal Shank	1	$0.25	$0.25		
Trim 2: 9 mm Antique Silver Metal Rivets	10	$0.10	$1.00		
Trim 3: Metal Zipper	1	$0.25	$0.25		
Freight: Vendor > Factory	1	$0.25	$0.25		
				$1.75	
Notions	Est. Quantity	@Est. $/yard/gr/pc	Est. Cost		
Notion 1: Thread	1	$1.00	$1.00		
Notion 2: Logo Back Patch	1	$0.50	$0.50		
Freight: Vendor > Factory	1	$0.25	$0.25		
				$1.75	**FRONT VIEW**
Labor	Direct	Contract Work			
Cutting: Domestic	$1.45				
Sewing: Domestic	$4.55				
Finishing: Domestic	$0.75				
Marking/ Grading: Domestic	$0.75				
				$7.50	
EST. First Cost of Goods				$25.66	
		Markup Goal %	100%– MU%	Markup $	
Selling Price					
					BACK VIEW

Cost Sheet 1: Traditional cost sheet- filled in sample; placed with Domestic

FINISHING: PRESSING, INSPECTING, LABELING, TAGGING, PACKING

Finishing is the final factor that goes into the FC. It is the final step before shipping, and it occurs once a garment has been sewn or knitted. The completely assembled garment moves to a finishing area for inspection, tagging, bagging, and/or boxing. The larger factories have different stations for pressing, inspecting, and packaging. Regardless of the factory size, once sewing is complete, garments are steamed or pressed, and then checked for errors or irregularities and any stray threads snipped. Next, each style gets its appropriate hang tags, price tags, plus extra yarn or buttons attached. Garments are folded and placed in poly bags or boxed, or they are put on hangers and bagged or boxed. These activities are grouped together as one line item, generally titled finishing, and are assigned one cost from the factory. There is rarely a cost breakdown; however, generally these costs are fairly low, most often about 15–20 percent of the labor costs.

Once all labor costs are calculated, they too go on to the cost sheet.

The aforementioned factors (fabric, trims, pattern-making, grading, marking, sewing, piecework, and finishing) are tallied up to arrive at the FC.

Next, we add the markup to arrive the wholesale price (or the selling price in a basic cost sheet scenario).

Markup

The markup is the amount above and beyond the FC to cover all overhead and selling expenses plus the desired profit amount. Markup is a dollar amount, and **markup percent** is a percentage of the FC that is added to arrive at the selling price.

Traditionally, a branded wholesaler doubles the FC to arrive at their wholesale price. In turn, the retailer doubles the wholesale price to arrive at the retail cost.

> First Cost × 2 = Wholesale Price   Wholesale Price × 2 = Retail Price
> $10.00 × 2 = $20.00 $20.00 × 2 = $40.00

This "doubling" is known as a **keystone** markup. When you keystone, you sell an item at twice the price at which it was produced or purchased. This is considered a 50 percent markup (two times the cost). The doubled amount is meant to cover any and all overhead expenses and profit. There are still a few companies who swear by this simple formula. But most only use it as a quick guideline, and instead a majority of companies use a markup percent ranging from 35 percent to 70 percent. The percent will vary based on the quantity produced, quantity ordered, fashion level, risk level, or by the perceived value.

When calculating markup, a manufacturer adds a markup to their FC to arrive at the wholesale price. A retailer adds markup to the wholesale cost to arrive at the retail price.

When you calculate markup, you insert your FC and desired markup percent (MU) into this equation:

> [C ÷ (100 − MU)] × 100 = $ Price

When you keystone, if the item costs $10.00, you insert 50 percent as the markup. Therefore the equation looks like this:

> [**$10.00** ÷ (100 − **50**)] × 100 = $ Price
> [$10.00 ÷ 50] × 100 = $ Price
> 0.2 × 100 = $20.00

Fifty percent is the markup percent and $10.00 is the markup in dollars.

Technically, when a keystone markup is used, it is a 100 percent markup. However, in fashion, we refer to keystone as a 50 percent markup, because 50 percent of the $20.00 wholesale or retail selling price is $10.00.

Although markups vary from 30 percent to 70 percent, most often the range is narrower, and you find companies working with a 46 percent to 60 percent markup.

A 46 percent markup is calculated like this:

$$[\textbf{\$10.00} \div (100 - \textbf{46})] \times 100 = \$ \text{ Sell Price}$$
$$[\$10.00 \div 54] \times 100 = \$ \text{ Sell Price}$$
$$0.185 \times 100 = \$18.50$$

$8.50 is the markup in dollars.

A 60 percent markup on a $10.00 item is calculated like this:

$$[\textbf{\$10.00} \div (100 - \textbf{60})] \times 100 = \$ \text{ Sell Price}$$
$$[\$10.00 \div 40] \times 100 = \$ \text{ Sell Price}$$
$$0.25 \times 100 = \$25.00$$

There is more than one way to calculate markup. Another way to easily figure markup is calculated with less steps, and is also commonly utilized. To determine a 60 percent markup on a $10.00 item, you divide your cost price by 100 percent minus your markup, then convert the percentage to a decimal by moving the decimal point two spaces over to the left. See the following example:

$$\$10.00 / (100\% - 60\%) = \$ \text{ Sell Price}$$
$$\$10.00 / 40\% = \$ \text{ Sell Price}$$
$$\$10.00 / 0.40 = \$25.00$$

$15.00 is the markup in dollars. You can check the markup dollar calculation by following this formula:

Selling Price $ – Cost Price $ = Markup Dollars $

To cross check your work and ensure the markup percent is accurate, you calculate backwards from the selling prices and cost.

$$(\text{Sell Price} - \text{Cost Price}) / (\text{Sell Price}) = \text{Markup Percentage } \%$$
$$(\$25.00 - \$10.00) / (\$25.00) = \text{Markup Percentage } \%$$
$$\$15.00 / \$25.00 = 0.6$$
$$0.6 = \text{Markup Percentage } \%$$
$$\text{Markup Percentage} = 60\%$$

There are times you may wish to sell an item at a particular price and you know your target. With that information, you can figure out your target cost. You work backwards from your desired selling price and markup goal. For example, you desire to sell an item at $25.00 as given earlier. You do not know your target cost yet, but you would like to have a markup goal of 60 percent.

Target Cost $ = Selling Price $ × (100% – Markup Goal %)
Target Cost $ = $25.00 × (100% – 60%)
Target Cost $ = $25.00 × (40%)
Remember, then convert your percentage by moving the decimal point over two spaces to the left.
Target Cost $ = $25.00 × .40
Target Cost $ = $10.00

In addition to the these shortcuts, here is a way to figure out your markup percentage if you know your target cost and your intended selling price.

Markup % = (Selling Price $ – Cost Price $) / Selling Price
Remember $25.00 – $10.00 are your Markup $ when you subtract the Selling Price $ – Cost Price $
Markup % = ($25.00 – $10.00) / $25.00
Markup % = $15.00 / $25.00
Markup % = .60
Then, convert the decimal to a percentage by moving over the decimal point two spaces over to the right
Markup % = 60%

Now You Figure Out The Prices!

1. Your item costs $25 to make. You have a markup goal of 55 percent. What would be the selling price?

2. You are creating a basic pocket T-shirt with a factory, and the total fabric costs are $5.00. The total trim costs are $0.75 and the total labor costs are $1.50. You have a markup goal of 65 percent. What is the selling price of your T-shirt?

3. You have a pair of trousers that you are aiming to sell at $45.00. You need to figure out your target cost. In addition, you would like to sell your trousers at a 70 percent markup goal. What would be the target cost of your trousers?

4. The cost price of your sweatshirt is $9.00. You want to sell your sweatshirt at $27.00. What is the markup percentage goal for this item?

5. You are planning to produce a dress style with a manufacturer. The total fabric costs are $12.00. The total trim costs are $2.55 and the total labor costs are $6.25. Your markup goal is 50 percent. What is the selling price of your dress style?

Once a style is sold at wholesale, the retailer needs to keystone again. However, in most cases, a keystone markup is not sufficient to cover all expenses, overhead costs, and a sustainable profit, as well as any coupons or discounts that may be applied to each sale. Therefore, a retailer generally marks the wholesale price up 55–65 percent to cover all the aforementioned factors.

If you do not plan to sell wholesale, and instead sell direct to the consumer, you must add a slightly higher markup. **Direct-to-consumer** markups generally fall in the 65 percent and 75 percent range, as there is no middle person, and the designer gets a slightly higher markup to cover time/expenses for shipping many individual products, as per selling many quantities at a time to retailers (see Table 2.5). There will be more of this costing information in Chapter 6.

What Needs to Be Paid from Profit Markup?

Whether a business uses a keystone or any other markup percent, all operating expenses need to be paid out of this markup and the profit must come out of this markup as well.

The expenses that must be covered by the markup include payroll, rent, insurance, taxes, utilities, office supplies, marketing expenses, sales commissions, photography, postage, web fees, accounting fees, and any trade show or other selling/promotional costs. This is not a complete list, as everything must be paid out of the markup money.

In the past, traditional costing worked well as it was easy to oversee and chart all expenses. Supply chains were not as complex as they are today, and were generally local-based. The selling periods were longer, and the chances of styles selling at full price were therefore higher. Direct costs (in terms of local labor and materials) were higher, so doubling the FC (or cost of goods) made complete sense, as there was a hefty amount of markup to cover the long list of expenses and still have a good amount leftover as earnings. Traditional costing is fairly easy to calculate and is beneficial since the costing process is simplified. Traditional costing allows for and easy comparison of unit costs. It is still used today, mainly for pre-production—as a quick check for a ballpark price—as well as by many young companies that are producing locally or domestically and have a full hand-in most steps of the design and production. Thus, in this manner, costing has changed. What has changed so much, and why the simple keystone formula no longer suffices, is that today most production is overseas. Global production involves many parties. We find ourselves with a complex supply chain, not fully transparent from our home countries. This new model creates parts of the supply chain that add more costs—some quite easy to track, and others more difficult to see—and to comprehend and calculate how and where they should be included on a cost sheet. Although overseas production allows for lower-priced costs of goods, it does make the costing process more complicated and laborious.

Summary

Traditional costing includes the basics: material costs, plus labor and profit. FC, also referred to as direct costs, are the materials and labor added with the desired markup. Materials include fabric, lining, trim, notions, and so on. Labor includes pattern making, cutting, sewing, tagging, packing, and any other direct labor costs. FC are only done if a sample is available. If no sample is available, refer to a similar past style's post-production cost sheet for reference. Fabric is normally the greatest cost. Each fabric must be listed separately on the cost sheet showing the fabric yield or fabric consumption—the amount of fabric needed for each style. The yield is multiplied by the cost to determine the cost of the fabric. All fabric information must be list on the Bill of Materials (BOM), a page within the tech pack.

Table 2.5 Step 5—Apply markup to first cost to calculate selling price

CREATING A COST SHEET

Now that you have your Total First Cost of Goods, you must apply the markup to this to land at your direct-to-consumer selling price!

Take the FC of Goods and divide it by the balance of your Markup Goal subtracted from 100%

In this case, the FC is $25.66

The Markup Goal is 65%

Therefore, you will divide the First Cost by 35%

(100% – 65%)

Remember to follow this simple formula

Selling Price = First Cost / (100% – Markup Goal)

Selling Price = $25.66 / (100% – 65%)

Selling Price = $25.66 / 35%

Remember to move the decimal point over 2 places to the left to convert a % to a decimal (.)

Selling Price = $25.66 / .35 = $73.30

Selling Price ⟹

Preliminary Basic Cost Sheet					
Date 03/10/2021		**Company** KRV Designs			
Style No. 1111	**Sxs No.** 210	**Season** Spring Delivery 1		**Group** Men's Denim Bottoms	
Size Range 28-36	**Sxs Size** 32	**Description** 5-Pocket Denim Jean Relaxed Fit Jean			
Fabric 14 Oz 100% Cotton Denim - 60"					
Fabric	Est. Yield	@Est. $/ yard	Est. Cost	Total Est. Cost	**SKETCHES**
Fabric 1: 14 oz Denim	2	$6.99	$13.98		
Fabric 2: Plainweave	0.125	$1.40	$0.18		
Freight: Mill > Factory	1	$0.50	$0.50		
				$14.66	
Trims	Est. Quantity	@Est. $/ yard/gr/pc	Est. Cost		
Trim 1: 20 mm Antique Silver Metal Shank	1	$0.25	$0.25		
Trim 2: 9 mm Antique Silver Metal Rivets	10	$0.10	$1.00		
Trim 3: Metal Zipper	1	$0.25	$0.25		
Freight: Vendor > Factory	1	$0.25	$0.25		
				$1.75	
Notions	Est. Quantity	@Est. $/ yard/gr/pc	Est. Cost		
Notion 1: Thread	1	$1.00	$1.00		
Notion 2: Logo Back Patch	1	$0.50	$0.50		
Freight: Vendor > Factory	1	$0.25	$0.25		
				$1.75	
Labor	Direct	Contract Work			
Cutting: China	$1.45				
Sewing: China	$4.55				
Finishing: China	$0.75				
Marking/ Grading: China	$0.75				
				$7.50	**FRONT VIEW**
EST. First Cost of Goods				$25.66	
		Markup Goal %	100%– MU%	Markup $	
		65%	35%	$47.65	
Selling Price				$73.30	
					BACK VIEW

Sample sizes are used on the traditional cost sheet to base the fabric consumption. Sample sizes are used for fittings, style revisions, selling, and approvals. The same sample size will be used for each style, and it is typically the middle size in the size range. The size range will greatly affect fabric consumption and cost. This is especially true if a great amount of large sizes are produced. Breaking down a wide range of sizes into petite, regular, and large sizes will give a more accurate cost.

Fabric is produced in a variety of different widths, which affects the marker and fabric yield. Fabric layout, print, and direction must be taken into account when creating a marker, and it will affect the fabric yield. Trim costs such as zippers, buttons, labels, and so on are calculated into the FC. These are purchased in bulk in a variety of different units, quantities, and measurements. The amount of trim or findings per style is multiplied by the cost to determine the cost of each. Shipping fabric, trims, and findings are all included in the FC.

Direct labor costs include pattern making, marker making, cutting, sewing, pressing, labeling, and more. Bill of Labor (BOL) is used to record all direct labor activities, and it is calculated by multiplying the time in the minutes or hours it takes to perform the task by the hourly or daily rate a worker is paid. The pattern maker, also known as a garment engineer, develops the initial pattern, makes adjustments after fittings, and creates the final production pattern. Grading is the shrinking or enlargement of a production pattern to create different sizes. The grader takes direction from the pattern maker, who supplies a specification sheets with measurements and grade rules. Marker making is performed once the pattern and fabric is finalized. The marker can greatly affect the fabric yield, and therefore the cost of the garment.

Cutting occurs when fabric is spread across the cutting table, and pattern pieces or markers are laid to eliminate the surrounding excess fabric. Cutting cost is calculated by multiplying the cutting time by the cutter's wages, and then divided by the number of styles being cut at one time. Factory-sewing costs are calculated by determining how long it takes to sew each detail and seam. Most often, an entire garment is not sewn by one person and therefore all steps are timed separately and added together. SAMs are determined and multiplied by the sewers average wage. The more complex the garment, the longer it will take to complete. Piece work, trimming, and embellishments, such as screen printing, beading, and so on may take place in another part of the factory or an entirely different factory. The cost of labor and often the logistics must be added into the cost for this process. Finishing, pressing, inspecting, labeling, tagging, and packing are the final factors that are added into the FC. These actions rarely have a cost breakdown but most often are about 15–20 percent of the labor costs.

Markup is the amount added to the FC to cover overhead and selling expenses as well as the desired profit amount. Calculated in both dollar amount and percent, when added to the FC, it will result in the selling price. Wholesalers typically double the FC to arrive at the wholesale price, also known as the keystone. Markups usually range between 30 percent and 70 percent. Once sold at wholesale, the retailer again adds a markup to cover expenses, overhead costs, and profit.

Chapter Review and Discussion

1. Why do you think the largest percent of FC is the price of the fabric?
2. Why do fashion designers and manufacturers apply different markups to different styles? Why might they apply different markups at different times of the year? And, then why might they decide to adjust a markup for a particular retailer?
3. What are some of the different factors that influence building a size range, the size scale, and your sample size for your collection? If you are a women's apparel brand and are looking to branch out into the inclusive-sizing market, what steps would you take to execute your pre-production methods and plan your sizing for this new inclusive-size division?

Activities and Exercises

1. You find a wool tweed fabric for US$12.00 per yard/meter and decide to use it for a new skirt style that requires 1.5 yards/meters of the tweed. You add a side-seam zipper at $1.50/piece and one 24L button at the waistline tab above the zipper. The button you select costs $43.00/gross. The skirt is unlined and a local factory gives you a CMT price of $10.50/skirt. You are producing 300 of the style. What other costs do you need in order to calculate the FC? Research wholesale prices of those items and determine what is the FC for this tweed skirt style. What will your selling price be if you use the keystone formula for markup? What will your price be if you apply a 55 percent markup? And if you apply a 64 percent markup?

2. You are a merchandiser for women's woven apparel. A new style button-down shirt was introduced into the current collection as a fashion item. However, due to the great success of this style selling, your team decides that they will like to carry it over to future seasons using a new fabric appropriate for the season. How will this affect your costing? In addition, you want to increase your markup on this style. What are some ways to achieve an increase on achieving a better markup?

3. You are asked to compare two similar apparel items from two completely different brands. One style comes from a high fashion, luxury designer brand. The other style is from a mass market and is much lower-priced point apparel item. Please list out the major differences regarding what makes these two items different in price and quality. Take into consideration the following factors; construction details, fabric, trims, sewing, labor costs, etc.

Key Terms

direct cost	markup
direct-to-consumer	markup percent
fabric consumption	point of measure
fabric yield	SAMs (standard allowed minutes)
FC (first cost)	self-fabric
keystone	sloper

ANSWERS FOR QUESTIONS ON PAGE 32

1. $25.00/0.45 = $55.55 Selling Price

2. ($5.00 + $0.75 + $1.50) / (100% − 65%) = $20.71 Selling Price

3. $45 x (100% − 70%) = $13.50 Target Cost

4. ($27.00 − $9.00) / $27.00 = 0.67 or 67 Markup %

5. ($12.00 + $2.55 + $6.25) / (100% − 50%) = $41.60 Selling Price

3 Global Production Sourcing and Costing

Introduction

Today over 90 percent of garments sold in the United States are made elsewhere around the globe. Fibers are grown and textiles are produced worldwide, as well as all trims and notions are manufactured globally. The textile and trimmings are shipped to apparel-making factories throughout the world. The majority of these factories are in Central and South Asia, mainly in China, India, and Bangladesh. There are 195 countries on Earth, and all 195 countries produce apparel (Birnbaum 2008).

Brands slowly started moving production to many of these 195 countries three or four decades ago, but in the last twenty years, there was a major shift, and suddenly the majority of production moved overseas, where labor and many material costs are considerably lower. Overseas labor costs specifically are a small fraction of the cost of equivalent labor in the United States, where sewers are paid $95.00/day on average. Garment labor rates overseas often equate to just about $1.50/hour (Lu 2018). Search online for "Sheng Lu fashion, FASH455", or follow the QR code for more details.

Daily Wages for Garment Workers in 2017 Based on 5.5 days/week	
Country	Average Daily Rate (in US$)
Bangladesh	$8.56
China	$11.73
El Salvador	$17.96
India	$11.08
Indonesia	$10.04
Mexico	$9.00
Pakistan	$13.91
Philippines	$16.17
Sri Lanka	$8.43
Vietnam	$10.78

Source: Sheng Lu Fashion 2018.

In terms of costing, moving production abroad allowed brands to lower their pricing. Companies had to place orders earlier due to the lengthened shipping time and brands had to order increased quantities, but it was thought that the far lower labor costs were worth the longer lead times and the larger batches. This model, although initially exciting, caused fashion companies to often commit to orders larger than they needed. As more companies also moved their production overseas, a larger amount of garments overall were created, leaving many as unsold inventory. Sales, which were historically seasonal, became a regular occurrence. This is why we currently find a large clearance section in many retail stores at all times and a plethora of discounters filled with racks of marked-down, excess, and imported fashions.

This shift to overseas production is slowly reversing. A mix of wage increases for garment workers, particularly in China, combined with a slowly increasing amount of consumers preferring "Made in USA" products, has reduced that amount of overseas garment production from 95 percent in 2015 to 92 percent in 2018.

This said, we are still at a point in time where the bulk of apparel is produced overseas.

Costing apparel that is not produced in your neighborhood, city, or state adds many cost factors. Let's take a look at how today's global production methods affect costing.

Effects of Global Production on Costing

The same cost factors involved in traditional apparel costing—fabric, trims, labor, shipping, and markup—are key components no matter where production takes place. However, when producing internationally, there are additional cost considerations, which include **direct sourcing** (when a company staff member travels overseas and visits the factories and suppliers oneself), buying office or **sourcing agent** fees, ocean/air freight, insurance, port security charges, crating fees, duty, customs clearance and customs broker fees, off-loading fees, additional transport fees, and warehouse storage. These fees can total close to the amount of your first cost or, depending how you ship, even more. To understand those fees, it is important to discuss how prices from international suppliers and factories are advised.

International Costing Terms

Depending on the **COO** in which the materials/goods will be manufactured, the price advised may or may not include delivery to your factory or home-country office. For international goods, prices are quoted in several ways. A supplier may advise the cost to simply manufacture the goods, or they may advise the price and include delivery of the items to your door, or perhaps halfway there. There are standard abbreviations placed after the cost in a cost quotation that explain whether there will be an additional expense to get the goods to your factory. If so, then freight and taxes will need to be entered on the cost sheet.

These abbreviated terms, known as the **Incoterms®** Rules, are universal, and are used for determining pricing for manufacturing, importing, and exporting. These universal rules define the responsibilities of the sellers and buyers for the delivery of goods under contract. They are published by the International Chamber of Commerce (ICC). Search online for "Export, Know Your Incoterms", which provides a useful overview and details on where to find more information on the Incoterms® Rules, or follow the QR code here.

When sourcing and selecting fabric, trim, materials, or garment production from overseas, you will know if each cost includes freight and insurance by the abbreviation that follows the price quotations from mills, factories, and suppliers. If there are no Incoterms® Rules included with a price quote, then be aware that there are many additional fees to pay.

These abbreviated terms accompanying prices for overseas materials and products allow you to know if freight and other services are included. They are:

- **X-FTY** or **ExW** (Ex-Factory or Ex-Works): This is only cost of the goods to be manufactured. X-FTY and/or ExW do not include handling, shipping, or taxes. The responsibility of the manufacturer of the goods ends at the factory's outgoing door.
- **FAS** (Free Alongside): This price includes the cost of the goods to be manufactured and then delivered to the port, loading dock, etc. The cost does not include uploading to the ship, plane, or truck; shipping; or taxes. The responsibility of the manufacturer of the goods ends at when it is delivered to the shipper.
- **FOB** (Free on Board): The cost of the goods to be manufactured, delivered to the port or loading dock, and uploaded to the ship, plane, or truck. The cost does not include shipping or taxes. The responsibility of the manufacturer of the goods ends at when the goods are loaded onto the shipping vessel.
- **CIF** (Cost, Insurance, and Freight): The cost of the goods to be manufactured; delivered to the port or loading dock; uploaded to the ship, plane, or truck; and shipped with all applicable insurance fees included along the way. The cost does not include duties, clearing customs, or local shipping. The responsibility of the manufacturer of the goods ends when the goods arrive at the destination port.
- **DDP** (Delivered and Duty Paid): The cost of the goods to be manufactured, delivered to the port/loading dock, uploaded to the vessel, shipped, insured, offloaded from the vessel, brought through customs, with duties paid, loaded on to a local forwarder, and delivered to your warehouse/retailer/etc. The cost includes the goods being offloaded from the delivery truck and arriving at your door.

The above summaries provide a general introduction to the ICC Rules, however, please be aware of their limitations. If you are involved in establishing an Incoterms policy for your organisation, or in the drafting of contracts with trading partners or service providers, you should always refer to the most current text of Incoterms published by the ICC. Download the Incoterms app to receive the latest news and updates.

Now that you are aware of how your prices will be quoted, let's look at the various fees and costs that are incorporated in all those given terms. These factors include direct sourcing expenses, sourcing buying office and sourcing agent fees, freight forwarding, and customs fees.

Global production brings more line items on the cost sheet and has brought us to the common cost sheet in use today.

Table 3.1 Traditional apparel-industry cost sheet

Traditional Cost Sheet					
Date		Company			
Style No.	Sxs No.	Season			Group
Size Range	Sxs Size	Description			
Fabric					
Fabric	Est. Yield	@Est. $/yard	Est. Cost	Total Est. Cost	SKETCHES
Fabric 1:					
Fabric 2:					
Freight:					
Trims	Est. Quantity	@Est. $/yard/gr/pc	Est. Cost		
Trim 1:					
Trim 2:					
Trim 3:					
Freight:					FRONT VIEW
Notions	Est. Quantity	@Est. $/yard/gr/pc	Est. Cost		
Notion 1:					
Notion 2:					
Freight:					
Labor	Direct	Contract Work			
Cutting:					
Sewing:					
Finishing:					
Marking/Grading:					
EST. First Cost of Goods					
Agent Commission %					
Est. Freight					
Duty %					
Clearance %					BACK VIEW
Local Freight					
Total Misc Costs					
Est. LDP / DDP Cost					
Wholesale Markup		Markup Goal %	100%–MU%	Markup $	
Wholesale Price					
Retailer Markup		Markup Goal %	100%–MU%	Markup $	
Retailer Price					
Manufacturer's Suggested Retail Price (MSRP)					

Direct Factory Sourcing

Often when a brand is importing, they want to see firsthand the factories and suppliers that will be producing their materials and garments. Visiting these factories, whether overseas or over the border, can add up in terms of costs. Factory sourcing and research involves air travel, hotel bills, meals, and carfare to and from all the factories, and often includes interpreter fees. Expenses will add up if you also visit sourcing trade shows overseas and/or conduct inspections while in each factory. Direct sourcing costs money, as well as time and energy. It is a bit difficult to determine how direct sourcing becomes a line item on a cost sheet. However if, at the end of a China-sourcing trip, for instance, you have invested $5,000 for airfare, hotel, and all other costs, then those are costs that should be covered on a cost sheet. Simply letting those be covered by markup means that your markup percent has quite a bit to cover before it becomes profit. Often a company will add direct sourcing fees to the miscellaneous line on a cost sheet and divide their projected sourcing and similar costs by the number of total units projected and add that amount to their cost sheet. This is recommended, because, in the authors' opinions, when you are in the business of making blouses, pants, or hosiery and there are expenses related to producing those blouses, pants, or hosiery, then those expenses are blouse, pant, or hosiery cost factors. Dividing the cost of a production trip by the amount of **Stock Keeping Units** (**SKUs**) you plan to produce is not ideal, but remember, costing worksheets are working sheets. A SKU for a style is the amount of colors multiplied by the amount of sizes in a style. For instance, if a T-shirt comes in three colors (black, white, and navy) and is offered in sizes XS–XL (meaning XS, S, M, L, and XL), you have five sizes in the size range. The style SKU count would be fifteen because you multiply three colors by five sizes in this style. It is preferred to divide the direct sourcing expenses by total units produced.

Total spent on direct factory sourcing = $5,000.00
Total SKUs = 15
Average # units per SKU = 500
Total # units = 7,500

Direct Sourcing $ ÷ Total # units = Direct Sourcing $/style
$5,000.00 ÷ 7,500 = $0.6666
$0.67 per style can be added to the cost sheet to cover overseas sourcing trips

---

It is better to account for all costs than to leave large expenses off the costing sheet to be covered by the markup, as the markup must encompass so many other expenses. This will be addressed in length in Chapter 4.

Buying Office and Sourcing Agent Fees

A designer or brand may choose to hire a sourcing agent or order through a buying office. Sourcing agents and buying offices take care of sourcing and procuring materials and production factories as they have relationships with a large network of suppliers and manufacturers. Your buying office or agent is your eyes, ears, and voice in the factory, and can add a great value to your product. They take care of communications, quality assessments, and troubleshoot crises, errors, or delays if they arise. Buying offices often help with the development of your design and can complete tech packs, or approve **lab dips**. Lab dips are approval samples for fabrics and trims used for color matching and quality and weight testing. They can also provide other time-sensitive support.

LIM College adjunct professor, Juliette Creglia-Atwi, offered her thoughts on buying office fees during a telephone conversation: Before committing to work with a buying office, such as Li & Fung, senior management from the fashion company negotiates a fee with the buying office. The fee is a percent of the first cost or FOB. On average, a buying office or agent receives between 5 to 10%, and the agreed percent is applied to all orders for a contracted period of time. A large-sized company may negotiate a fee of 5–7%, while a smaller company's fee will likely be in the 8–10% range.

During pre-production costing, it is recommended you estimate agent's fee using the higher percent of the range. Agents and buying offices are quite valuable when they are good at their jobs. They work, on your behalf, with your suppliers and factories. They interact with management and represent you to the factory management. Building relationships over a course of years is instrumental for the line's long-term success. This should be considered when first negotiating sourcing agent fees. It is recommended to not negotiate too low as doing so could set the relationship off on the wrong path.

Whether the agent/buying office's fee is a percent of FOB, CIF, or FC, depends on your price quotation. The commission is added at the point when the agent/buying office's responsibility ends.

Freight Forwarding Charges

Next, let's look at the costs incurred when floating or flying the finished production across the world to the home country. Depending on the price you are quoted from your manufacturer or buying office, the price may or may not include ocean or air freight. If you or a **freight forwarder**—someone who organizes transportation of goods—are arranging the shipping, you want to make sure you receive an all-inclusive international freight price. Otherwise, there are many assorted fees in which you may be billed, including documentation fees, crating and pallet fees, off-loading and port security charges, terminal fees, value-added tax (VAT) for Chinese goods, warehouse storage fees, and cargo insurance extras for insuring from the port to final destination. The freight fees are variable, and your price quotation will be based on shipping distance, desired shipping time, and order value, volume, and weight. Therefore, it is difficult to estimate all-inclusive freight charges, especially because there are additional charges incurred that add up, such as $35–$75 USD per order (equal to $0.03–$0.07/per piece) added on average simply to cover paperwork and miscellaneous expenses for the order. This is above and beyond the actual freight charge (Noah 2017). Also, the quotation could increase if the shipment is late, as delayed cargo fees are then incurred. Once a shipment arrives at the destination seaport or airport, then there is an inland delivery charge to have it shipped to the final destination (i.e., the warehouse/office/store). That fee may or may not be included in your freight quote; therefore, it is important to learn if your price quote includes port-to-port or port-to-door (final destination) charges.

Table 3.2 Here is the traditional cost sheet filled out for jean KRV-1111 which includes 5% agent's commission added to the first cost

Traditional Cost Sheet					
Date 03/10/2021		**Company** KRV Designs			
Style No. 1111	**Sxs No.** 210	**Season** Spring Delivery 1		**Group** Men's Denim Bottoms	
Size Range 28–36	**Sxs Size** 32	**Description** 5-Pocket Denim Jean Relaxed Fit Jean			
Fabric 14 Oz 100% Cotton Denim–60"					
Fabric	**Est. Yield**	**@Est. $/yard**	**Est. Cost**	**Total Est. Cost**	**SKETCHES**
Fabric 1: 14 oz Denim	2	$6.99	$13.98		
Fabric 2: Plainweave	0.125	$1.40	$0.18		
Freight: Mill > Factory	1	$0.50	$0.50		
				$14.66	
Trims	**Est. Quantity**	**@Est. $/ yard/gr/pc**	**Est. Cost**		
Trim 1: 20 mm Antique Silver Metal Shank	1	$0.25	$0.25		
Trim 2: 9 mm Antique Silver Metal Rivets	10	$0.10	$1.00		
Trim 3: Metal Zipper	1	$0.25	$0.25		
Freight: Vendor > Factory	1	$0.25	$0.25		
				$1.75	
Notions	**Est. Quantity**	**@Est. $/ yard/gr/pc**	**Est. Cost**		
Notion 1: Thread	1	$1.00	$1.00		
Notion 2: Logo Back Patch	1	$0.50	$0.50		
Freight: Vendor > Factory	1	$0.25	$0.25		
				$1.75	**FRONT VIEW**
Labor	**Direct**	**Contract Work**			
Cutting: China	$1.45				
Sewing: China	$4.55				
Finishing: China	$0.75				
Marking/Grading: China	$0.75				
				$7.50	
EST. First Cost of Goods				$25.66	
Agent Commission %	5%			$1.28	
Est. Freight					
Duty %					
Clearance %					
Local Freight					
Total Misc Costs					
Est. LDP / DDP Cost					
Wholesale Markup		**Markup Goal %**	**100%– MU%**	**Markup $**	
Wholesale Price					
Retailer Markup		**Markup Goal %**	**100%– MU%**	**Markup $**	
Retailer Price					**BACK VIEW**
Manufacturer's Suggested Retail Price (MSRP)					

Table 3.3 Here is jean KRV-1111's cost sheet with international and local transportation costs added

Traditional Cost Sheet					
Date 03/10/2021		**Company** KRV Designs			
Style No. 1111	**Sxs No.** 210	**Season** Spring Delivery 1		**Group** Men's Denim Bottoms	
Size Range 28–36	**Sxs Size** 32	**Description** 5-Pocket Denim Jean Relaxed Fit Jean			
Fabric 14 Oz 100% Cotton Denim–60"					
Fabric	**Est. Yield**	**@Est. $/yard**	**Est. Cost**	**Total Est. Cost**	**SKETCHES**
Fabric 1: 14 oz Denim	2	$ 6.99	$13.98		
Fabric 2: Plainweave	0.125	$ 1.40	$0.18		
Freight: Mill > Factory	1	$ 0.50	$0.50		
				$14.66	
Trims	**Est. Quantity**	**@Est. $/ yard/gr/pc**	**Est. Cost**		
Trim 1: 20 mm Antique Silver Metal Shank	1	$0.25	$0.25		
Trim 2: 9 mm Antique Silver Metal Rivets	10	$0.10	$1.00		
Trim 3: Metal Zipper	1	$0.25	$0.25		
Freight: Vendor > Factory	1	$0.25	$0.25		
				$1.75	
Notions	**Est. Quantity**	**@Est. $/ yard/gr/pc**	**Est. Cost**		
Notion 1: Thread	1	$1.00	$1.00		
Notion 2: Logo Back Patch	1	$0.50	$0.50		
Freight: Vendor > Factory	1	$0.25	$0.25		
				$1.75	
Labor	**Direct**	**Contract Work**			FRONT VIEW
Cutting: China	$1.45				
Sewing: China	$4.55				
Finishing: China	$0.75				
Marking/Grading: China	$0.75				
				$7.50	
EST. First Cost of Goods				$25.66	
Agent Commission %	5%			$1.28	
Est. Freight	Boat			$0.65	
Duty %					
Clearance %					
Local Freight	Truck			$1.00	
Total Misc Costs					
Est. LDP / DDP Cost					
Wholesale Markup		**Markup Goal %**	**100%–MU%**	**Markup $**	
Wholesale Price					
Retailer Markup		**Markup Goal %**	**100%–MU%**	**Markup $**	
Retailer Price					BACK VIEW
Manufacturer's Suggested Retail Price (MSRP)					

Customs Clearance Fees

Once an order arrives at the sea or airport, it must pass through US Customs and Border Control. Getting the shipped order through US Customs incurs costs. Often a company hires a licensed customs broker to help in this regard. Customs brokers charge are a fee based on the volume of imports they bring in. The basic clearance fee for an imported volume for approximately 1,000 T-shirts port-to-door is US$150.00. This fee equates to 0.15/per style and excludes duties, bond, and all delivery and terminal fees, which are part of freight forwarding charges. It is somewhat difficult to know the exact customs broker fees until after the shipment has come through US Customs and been delivered. Past shipment information will help estimate this cost when filling in cost sheets.

An email interview questioning current brokerage practices and fees with customs broker Kenneth Blum of Northeastern Brokerage Company:

Q: Are we correct that when you import apparel you must hire a Licensed Customs Broker to clear customs, or can a brand/designer handle it all themselves?
A: If you want, you can have an in-house license broker on staff to handle imports for a corporation. For smaller companies, an individual can go thru the process as well. However, I do not recommend this because of the great time and effort involved, most companies hire a Customs Broker.

Q: Is the Licensed Customs Broker's fee a percent or a flat rate that is paid by the US brand?
A: Most charges are a flat-rate and they are based on the volume of imports.

Q: What is the basic flat rate for a small-to-mid-sized order?
A: The basic clearance fee is $150, that excludes bond, duties, delivery and terminal fees.

Q: What specifically does the Licensed Customs Broker take care of, please? (i.e., off-loading, customs clearance, duty, etc.)
A: They take care of all the various activities from door-to-door, door-to-port, or port-to-port. For example, for door-to-door the CB handles: pick-up freight, export for port clearance, import clearance, and delivery.

Q: How does hiring a CB affect cost?
A: The freight forwarder consolidates and passes along a rate that is lower than straight shipments, as they are shipping large volume. The rate varies. Commodity, weight, shipping dimensions, and value are all needed in order to determine a rate.

Table 3.4 Here is jean KRV-1111's cost sheet with international and local freight and custom's clearance fees added

Traditional Cost Sheet					
Date 03/10/2021		**Company** KRV Designs			
Style No. 1111	**Sxs No.** 210	**Season** Spring Delivery 1			**Group** Men's Denim Bottoms
Size Range 28–36	**Sxs Size** 32	**Description** 5-Pocket Denim Jean Relaxed Fit Jean			
Fabric 14 Oz 100% Cotton Denim–60"					
Fabric	**Est. Yield**	**@Est. $/yard**	**Est. Cost**	**Total Est. Cost**	**SKETCHES**
Fabric 1: 14 oz Denim	2	$6.99	$13.98		
Fabric 2: Plainweave	0.125	$1.40	$0.18		
Freight: Mill > Factory	1	$0.50	$0.50		
				$14.66	
Trims	**Est. Quantity**	**@Est. $/yard/gr/pc**	**Est. Cost**		
Trim 1: 20 mm Antique Silver Metal Shank	1	$0.25	$0.25		
Trim 2: 9 mm Antique Silver Metal Rivets	10	$0.10	$1.00		
Trim 3: Metal Zipper	1	$0.25	$0.25		
Freight: Vendor > Factory	1	$0.25	$0.25		
				$1.75	
Notions	**Est. Quantity**	**@Est. $/yard/gr/pc**	**Est. Cost**		
Notion 1: Thread	1	$1.00	$1.00		
Notion 2: Logo Back Patch	1	$0.50	$0.50		
Freight: Vendor > Factory	1	$0.25	$0.25		
				$1.75	
Labor	**Direct**	**Contract Work**			
Cutting: China	$1.45				
Sewing: China	$4.55				
Finishing: China	$0.75				
Marking/Grading: China	$0.75				
				$7.50	
EST. First Cost of Goods				$25.66	**FRONT VIEW**
Agent Commission %	5%			$1.28	
Est. Freight	Boat			$0.65	
Duty %					
Clearance %	2.5%			$0.64	
Local Freight	Truck			$1.00	
Total Misc Costs					
Est. LDP / DDP Cost					
Wholesale Markup		**Markup Goal %**	**100%–MU%**	**Markup $**	
Wholesale Price					
Retailer Markup		**Markup Goal %**	**100%–MU%**	**Markup $**	
Retailer Price					**BACK VIEW**
Manufacturer's Suggested Retail Price (MSRP)					

Duty

Separate from freight and customs fees is **duty**. Duties (also known as tariffs) are taxes imposed on goods produced outside of the home country (also known as the importing country). Duties are imposed when bringing the goods into the home country.

Freight and customs fees may or may not be the same line item on a cost sheet, but duty is always its own line item. Duty is a percent of the total cost of an imported product once it is landed, so FC, plus freight, insurance, and so on. Duty percentage rates vary quite a bit; the average tariffs on apparel vary from 10.8 percent to 14.2 percent (Belgum 2018), and the average duty on footwear is 11 percent. (Reagan 2018).

To determine the duty rate, consult the **US Harmonized Tariff Schedule (HTS)** list on the United States International Trade Commission's website (Visit https://www.usitc.gov or follow the QR code here). The HTS uses a numerical system for customs brokers to identify products and assign a duty rate percentage based on essential character. The HTS system classifies all types of goods from brooms, to apparel, to machinery. Each HTS code classification has six numbers.

- The first two digits indicate the chapter (or category), for example: Apparel and Clothing accessories; Knitted or Crocheted.
- The next two digits are the heading (or item type), for example: T-shirts, singlets, and other vests.
- The final two digits are the subheading (or fabrication in this case): cotton.

In this code: HS 610910, **61_ _ _ _** = Apparel and Clothing Accessories; Knitted or Crocheted; **6109_ _**= T-Shirts, singlets and other vests; and **610910**= made of cotton.

Tariffs vary depending on the HTS code. HTS category, heading, and subheading descriptions drill down to the fabrication and indicate what duty will be imposed. The schedule will also list any countries that have preferential trade agreements and therefore no duty. A good customs broker will specialize in certain categories. Manufacturers have been known to alter products to achieve lesser duty rates. For example, footwear importers will add a thin layer of felt to the bottom of the shoe to change the classification to slipper which has a lesser duty rate. Classification is to be taken seriously. Getting held up at customs for inaccurate paperwork, incorrect classification number, or incomplete paperwork will result in delays and increased expenses.

Once the goods have come through customs, and the freight, duties, and other fees have been paid, the goods are considered **landed.** The landed cost is the total cost of goods, plus all other expenses into and successfully through the port of destination. There are two types of landed costs: landed duty paid (LDP) and delivered duty paid (DDP). LDP is the traditional landed cost and is the total price of goods up to and through the port of destination. DDP is the total price of goods delivered to the final importer's specified destination. This can be to the warehouse, distribution center (DC), or direct to the retail store. DDP includes inland freight and the added insurance for this part of the product's journey. Insurance and any other incidental expenses that are needed along the journey of the garment are added together on a line item called Miscellaneous.

To reiterate, when producing outside of the home country, your cost includes several factors added to the first cost: agent or buying office commission, the sea or air and inland shipping charges, duty, customs clearance, insurance, and any miscellaneous expenses that hopefully will not may be incurred. Together these equal your landed cost.

Table 3.5 Here is jean KRV-1111's cost sheet now including the applicable duty rate

Traditional Cost Sheet					
Date 03/10/2021		**Company** KRV Designs			
				Group Men's Denim Bottoms	
Style No. 1111	**Sxs No.** 210	**Season** Spring Delivery 1			
Size Range 28–36	**Sxs Size** 32	**Description** 5-Pocket Denim Jean Relaxed Fit Jean			
Fabric 14 Oz 100% Cotton Denim–60"					
Fabric	**Est. Yield**	**@Est. $/yard**	**Est. Cost**	**Total Est. Cost**	**SKETCHES**
Fabric 1: 14 oz Denim	2	$6.99	$13.98		
Fabric 2: Plainweave	0.125	$1.40	$0.18		
Freight: Mill > Factory	1	$0.50	$0.50		
				$14.66	
Trims	**Est. Quantity**	**@Est. $/ yard/gr/pc**	**Est. Cost**		
Trim 1: 20 mm Antique Silver Metal Shank	1	$0.25	$0.25		
Trim 2: 9 mm Antique Silver Metal Rivets	10	$0.10	$1.00		
Trim 3: Metal Zipper	1	$0.25	$0.25		
Freight: Vendor > Factory	1	$0.25	$0.25		
				$1.75	
Notions	**Est. Quantity**	**@Est. $/ yard/gr/pc**	**Est. Cost**		
Notion 1: Thread	1	$1.00	$1.00		
Notion 2: Logo Back Patch	1	$0.50	$0.50		
Freight: Vendor > Factory	1	$0.25	$0.25		
				$1.75	**FRONT VIEW**
Labor	**Direct**	**Contract Work**			
Cutting: China	$1.45				
Sewing: China	$4.55				
Finishing: China	$0.75				
Marking/Grading: China	$0.75				
				$7.50	
EST. First Cost of Goods				**$25.66**	
Agent Commission %	5%			$1.28	
Est. Freight	Boat			$0.65	
Duty %	5%			$1.28	
Clearance %	2.5%			$0.64	
Local Freight	Truck			$1.00	
Total Misc Costs					
Est. LDP / DDP Cost					
Wholesale Markup		**Markup Goal %**	**100%–MU%**	**Markup $**	
Wholesale Price					
Retailer Markup		**Markup Goal %**	**100%–MU%**	**Markup $**	
Retailer Price					**BACK VIEW**
Manufacturer's Suggested Retail Price (MSRP)					

Table 3.6 Here is the cost sheet with agent's percent, transport, duty, and custom fees tallied for total miscellaneous costs

CREATING A COST SHEET

After adding up your Total First Cost, you must now factor in additional miscellaneous costs. These added costs can be anything like paying your overseas agent a commission fee, the freight costs or duty on imported goods.

Traditional Cost Sheet					
Date 03/10/2021		**Company** KRV Designs			
Style No. 1111	**Sxs No.** 210	**Season** Spring Delivery 1		**Group** Men's Denim Bottoms	
Size Range 28–36	**Sxs Size** 32	**Description** 5-Pocket Denim Jean Relaxed Fit Jean			
Fabric 14 Oz 100% Cotton Denim–60"					
Fabric	Est. Yield	@Est. $/ yard	Est. Cost	Total Est. Cost	**SKETCHES**
Fabric 1: 14 oz Denim	2	$6.99	$13.98		
Fabric 2: Plainweave	0.125	$1.40	$0.18		
Freight: Mill > Factory	1	$0.50	$0.50		
				$14.66	
Trims	Est. Quantity	@Est. $/ yard/gr/pc	Est. Cost		
Trim 1: 20 mm Antique Silver Metal Shank	1	$0.25	$0.25		
Trim 2: 9 mm Antique Silver Metal Rivets	10	$0.10	$1.00		
Trim 3: Metal Zipper	1	$0.25	$0.25		
Freight: Vendor > Factory	1	$0.25	$0.25		
				$1.75	
Notions	Est. Quantity	@Est. $/ yard/gr/pc	Est. Cost		
Notion 1: Thread	1	$1.00	$1.00		
Notion 2: Logo Back Patch	1	$0.50	$0.50		
Freight: Vendor > Factory	1	$0.25	$0.25		
				$1.75	
Labor	Direct	Contract Work			
Cutting: China	$1.45				**FRONT VIEW**
Sewing: China	$4.55				
Finishing: China	$0.75				
Marking/Grading: China	$0.75				
				$7.50	
EST. First Cost of Goods				$25.66	
Agent Commission %	5%			$1.28	
Est. Freight	Boat			$0.65	
Duty %	5%			$1.28	
Clearance %	2.5%			$0.64	
Local Freight	Truck			$1.00	
Total Misc Costs				$4.86	
Est. LDP / DDP Cost					
Wholesale Markup		Markup Goal %	100%– MU%	Markup $	
Wholesale Price					
Retailer Markup		Markup Goal %	100%– MU%	Markup $	
Retailer Price					**BACK VIEW**
Manufacturer's Suggested Retail Price (MSRP)					

Total Misc Cost

Table 3.7 Here the total first cost of jean KRV-1111 is added to the miscellaneous cost to calculate landed cost

CREATING A COST SHEET

Once all the miscellaneous costs are added up, you then take that Total Misc Cost plus the First Cost to get your LANDED COST

Agent Commission
+
Freight
+
Duty
+
Clearance
=
TOTAL MISC COST
First Cost
+
Total Misc Cost
=
LANDED COST

Traditional Cost Sheet					
Date 03/10/2021		**Company** KRV Designs			
				Group Men's	
Style No. 1111	**Sxs No.** 210	**Season** Spring Delivery 1		Denim Bottoms	
Size Range 28–36	**Sxs Size** 32	**Description** 5-Pocket Denim Jean Relaxed Fit Jean			
Fabric 14 Oz 100% Cotton Denim–60"					
Fabric	Est. Yield	@Est. $/ yard	Est. Cost	Total Est. Cost	**SKETCHES**
Fabric 1: 14 oz Denim	2	$6.99	$13.98		
Fabric 2: Plainweave	0.125	$1.40	$0.18		
Freight: Mill > Factory	1	$0.50	$0.50		
				$14.66	
Trims	Est. Quantity	@Est. $/ yard/gr/pc	Est. Cost		
Trim 1: 20 mm Antique Silver Metal Shank	1	$0.25	$0.25		
Trim 2: 9 mm Antique Silver Metal Rivets	10	$0.10	$1.00		
Trim 3: Metal Zipper	1	$0.25	$0.25		
Freight: Vendor > Factory	1	$0.25	$0.25		
				$1.75	
Notions	Est. Quantity	@Est. $/ yard/gr/pc	Est. Cost		
Notion 1: Thread	1	$1.00	$1.00		
Notion 2: Logo Back Patch	1	$0.50	$0.50		
Freight: Vendor > Factory	1	$0.25	$0.25		
				$1.75	
Labor	Direct	Contract Work			**FRONT VIEW**
Cutting: China	$1.45				
Sewing: China	$4.55				
Finishing: China	$0.75				
Marking/Grading: China	$0.75				
				$7.50	
EST. First Cost of Goods				$25.66	
Agent Commission %	5%			$1.28	
Est. Freight	Boat			$0.65	
Duty %	5%			$1.28	
Clearance %	2.5%			$0.64	
Local Freight	Truck			$1.00	
Total Misc Costs				$4.86	
Est. LDP / DDP Cost				$30.51	
Wholesale Markup		Markup Goal %	100%– MU%	Markup $	
Wholesale Price					
Retailer Markup		Markup Goal %	100%– MU%	Markup $	
Retailer Price					**BACK VIEW**
Manufacturer's Suggested Retail Price (MSRP)					

Landed Cost →

Table 3.8 In this cost sheet the wholesale markup is added to the landed cost

CREATING A COST SHEET

Now that you have your Landed Cost, you must calculate the Wholesale Markup and Wholesale Price.

If your goal is to markup the Landed Cost by 60%, then you must take 100% minus the Markup Goal %

In this case, the goal is 60%, so the balance left from 100% would be with 40%

From there, take your Landed Cost and divide it by the balance of your Markup Goal from 100% (40%)

CALCULATE YOUR MARKUP

$30.51 (LANDED COST)

Divided by

.40 (move the decimal point over 2 places to the left)

$30.51/.40 = $76.28

Wholesale ➡

Traditional Cost Sheet					
Date 03/10/2021		**Company** KRV Designs			
Style No. 1111	**Sxs No.** 210	**Season** Spring Delivery 1		**Group** Men's Denim Bottoms	
Size Range 28–36	**Sxs Size** 32	**Description** 5-Pocket Denim Jean Relaxed Fit Jean			
Fabric 14 Oz 100% Cotton Denim–60"					
Fabric	Est. Yield	@Est. $/ yard	Est. Cost	Total Est. Cost	**SKETCHES**
Fabric 1: 14 oz Denim	2	$6.99	$13.98		
Fabric 2: Plainweave	0.125	$1.40	$0.18		
Freight: Mill > Factory	1	$0.50	$0.50		
				$14.66	
Trims	Est. Quantity	@Est. $/ yard/gr/pc	Est. Cost		
Trim 1: 20 mm Antique Silver Metal Shank	1	$0.25	$0.25		
Trim 2: 9 mm Antique Silver Metal Rivets	10	$0.10	$1.00		
Trim 3: Metal Zipper	1	$0.25	$0.25		
Freight: Vendor > Factory	1	$0.25	$0.25		
				$1.75	
Notions	Est. Quantity	@Est. $/ yard/gr/pc	Est. Cost		
Notion 1: Thread	1	$1.00	$1.00		
Notion 2: Logo Back Patch	1	$0.50	$0.50		
Freight: Vendor > Factory	1	$0.25	$0.25		
				$1.75	
Labor	Direct	Contract Work			**FRONT VIEW**
Cutting: China	$1.45				
Sewing: China	$4.55				
Finishing: China	$0.75				
Marking/Grading: China	$0.75				
				$7.50	
EST. First Cost of Goods				$25.66	
Agent Commission %	5%			$1.28	
Est. Freight	Boat			$0.65	
Duty %	5%			$1.28	
Clearance %	2.5%			$0.64	
Local Freight	Truck			$1.00	
Total Misc Costs				$4.86	
Est. LDP / DDP Cost				$30.51	
Wholesale Markup		Markup Goal %	100%– MU%	Markup $	
		60%	40%	$45.77	
Wholesale Price				$76.28	
Retailer Markup		Markup Goal %	100%– MU%	Markup $	
Retailer Price					**BACK VIEW**
Manufacturer's Suggested Retail Price (MSRP)					

Global Production Sourcing and Costing 51

Table 3.9 In this cost sheet for jean KRV-111 the retail markup is added to the wholesale price to determine suggested retail selling price

CREATING A COST SHEET

After calculating your Wholesale Markup and Wholesale Price, you must now get to your Retail Price.

Follow the same steps as finding your Wholesale Price to get the Retail Price

If the retailer markup is 50%, then 100%-50% is 50%

Divide the Wholesale Price by the balance of the Retail Markup from 100%

CALCULATE YOUR MARKUP

$76.28 (WHOLESALE PRICE)

Divided by 50%

.50 (move the decimal point over 2 places to the left)

$76.28/.50 = $152.56

Then, ROUND UP the final retail price so it is a flat number or a pricing strategy that is aligned with your brand's pricing

Does your brand end their pricing with .00, .50, or .99?

Traditional Cost Sheet					
Date 03/10/2021		**Company** KRV Designs			
					Group Men's Denim Bottoms
Style No. 1111	**Sxs No.** 210	**Season** Spring Delivery 1			
Size Range 28–36	**Sxs Size** 32	**Description** 5-Pocket Denim Jean Relaxed Fit Jean			
Fabric 14 Oz 100% Cotton Denim–60"					
Fabric	Est. Yield	@Est. $ /yard	Est. Cost	Total Est. Cost	**SKETCHES**
Fabric 1: 14 oz Denim	2	$6.99	$13.98		
Fabric 2: Plainweave	0.125	$1.40	$0.18		
Freight: Mill > Factory	1	$0.50	$0.50		
				$14.66	
Trims	Est. Quantity	@Est. $/ yard/gr/pc	Est. Cost		
Trim 1: 20 mm Antique Silver Metal Shank	1	$0.25	$0.25		
Trim 2: 9 mm Antique Silver Metal Rivets	10	$0.10	$1.00		
Trim 3: Metal Zipper	1	$0.25	$0.25		
Freight: Vendor > Factory	1	$0.25	$0.25		
				$1.75	
Notions	Est. Quantity	@Est. $/ yard/gr/pc	Est. Cost		
Notion 1: Thread	1	$1.00	$1.00		
Notion 2: Logo Back Patch	1	$0.50	$0.50		
Freight: Vendor > Factory	1	$0.25	$0.25		
				$1.75	**FRONT VIEW**
Labor	Direct	Contract Work			
Cutting: China	$1.45				
Sewing: China	$4.55				
Finishing: China	$0.75				
Marking/Grading: China	$0.75				
				$7.50	
EST. First Cost of Goods				$25.66	
Agent Commission %	5%			$1.28	
Est. Freight	Boat			$0.65	
Duty %	5%			$1.28	
Clearance %	2.5%			$0.64	
Local Freight	Truck			$1.00	
Total Misc Costs				$4.86	
Est. LDP / DDP Cost				$30.51	
Wholesale Markup		Markup Goal %	100%- MU%	Markup $	
		60%	40%	$45.77	
Wholesale Price				$76.28	
Retailer Markup		Markup Goal %	100%- MU%	Markup $	
		50%	50%	$76.28	
Retailer Price				$152.56	**BACK VIEW**
Manufacturer's Suggested Retail Price (MSRP)				$155.00	

Retail

Markup is then applied to the landed cost of an item to arrive at the selling price. As illustrated here, utilizing the basic keystone markup formula:

$$\text{Landed Cost} \times 2 = \text{Wholesale Price}$$
$$\$12.00 \times 2 = \$24.00$$

When you produce overseas or over-the-border, and you are not living in the country, the network and supply chain becomes complex and less transparent. Those complexities and translucencies can lead to errors, oversights, and duplicity of steps. Although labor is less expensive when producing overseas, costs may incur if a production batch has an issue and you have to fly on a plane to a factory to troubleshoot when something goes wrong. This can erode at profit margin and make goods more expensive than domestic production. This is another reason all overseas and sourcing trips should be placed on a cost sheet, as discussed earlier in this chapter. Quality control is key, and with global production, it occurs far from your eyes. Therefore, it is imperative to approve quality from concept and development through every step of production, so errors are caught early on and great rework costs are avoided.

Today's technology has helped alleviate many of these errors as well has shortened the development time. Software programs such as **Enterprise Resource Planning (ERP)** and PLM programs help manufacturers have visibility across the production and development supply chains. ERP software is used to help manufacturers share and access information across the creation and distribution cycles of a style. PLM is an excellent resource to utilize in today's industry, as it works in a real-time communication setting helping to minimize timing and streamline communication. By using this sophisticated system, merchandisers, designers, and production managers can stay connected all around the world. PLM organizes all the components of a style in a series of folders with workflow pages. The main purpose is to break down all the attributes of a particular garment and what is needed to create this style at the production level. By using PLM, all partners in the supply chain process can access this information, make updates to the style folder, and efficiently organize this information. In order to convey this essential style information, a PLM software program will contain the following elements of information: style numbers, style flat sketches or colorway Computer-Aided Designs (CADs), style descriptions, fabric information, costing, pitch sheets, color palettes, a bill of materials, a BOL, construction details, measurement specifications, and any reference or inspirational images to help better describe the requirements for the final outcome of the production of your garment. Another great feature to the PLM program is that if your global partners do not have PLM, you can export the information input into the database system into a pdf file to create a technical package. From there, you can send this tech pack via email or print hard copies of this pdf file to support the garment- or sample-making process! The style folders given here were created using the Gerber YuniquePLM® software. Search online for "YuniquePLM", or follow the QR code for further details.

However, it is important to know that not all companies use PLM, as it is sometimes quite an expensive software to purchase. Many do their costing in Excel and are quite satisfied with their performance and the low-cost-advantage of Excel compared to PLM programs.

Global production has undoubtedly allowed the fashion industry to make more garments at far lower prices. Lower costs are the main reason why so many brands produce overseas today. To keep those costs so sharp, it is important to research and assemble as transparent a supply chain as possible, so your low-cost styles arrive the way you specified. Otherwise you will pay in many ways to rework them, or they will be discounted; either way that is a profit loss, and they will no longer be low-cost styles. Keeping production in home countries, although much pricier in terms of costs of production, involves less time and cost factors to calculate, a more transparent supply chain, and any compliance issues are caught and resolved easier without overseas travel/hotel costs.

Fig. 3.1 Here is the digital style folder for jean KRV-1111 using the Gerber YuniquePLM® Version 8 program.

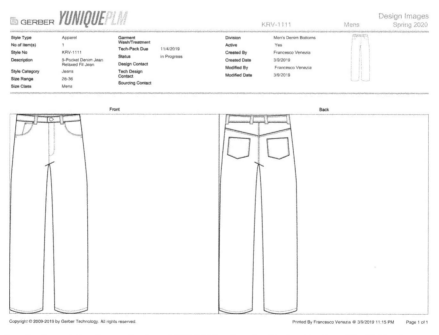

Fig. 3.2 Here is a tech pack lead page for jean KRV-1111 using the Gerber YuniquePLM® Version 8 program.

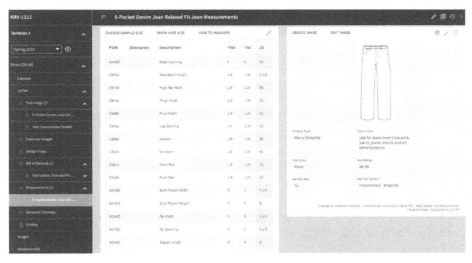

Fig. 3.3 Here is a Measurement Specifications sheet for jean KRV-1111 using the Gerber YuniquePLM® Version 8 program.

Summary

Global production has primarily moved overseas due to lower labor costs. This has given rise to brands ordering larger quantities, resulting in longer lead times. Having to commit to larger orders created large amounts of unsold inventory. This excess inventory is evident in the many discount racks. This trend is reversing as wages increase abroad, particularly in China, and consumers are seeking Made-in-USA products.

The effects of global production on costing has resulted in additional costs to consider such as direct sourcing, buying office or sourcing agent fees, ocean/air freight, insurance, port security charges, crating fees, additional transport fees, and warehouse storage. These costs can total the same amount as first costs or more. In addition, the use of PLM software may also be an added cost due to the high costs of acquiring this sophisticated software.

Direct factory sourcing can be costly due to the fact that factories and suppliers must be visited. Air travel, hotel bills, meals, carfare, interpreters, and trade shows must be accounted for, but is difficult to determine how to include on a line sheet. Adding direct sourcing fees as a miscellaneous line in the cost sheet is advised instead of allowing the markup to cover costs.

Buying office and sourcing agent fees are an agreed percentage ranging from 5 percent to 10 percent, depending on how large the firm is. The sourcing agents are responsible for sourcing, procuring materials, and communicating with production factories, and they also ensure quality assessment and troubleshoot any crises, errors, or delays. It is recommended to view your sourcing agent as an investment by not negotiating too low a fee. The sourcing agents fee can be based off the FOB or first costs.

Freight forwarders arrange shipping and should organize an all-inclusive international freight price. Freight forwarding charges may or may not be included in the price quoted by the manufacturer or buying office. These fees include documentation, crating, and pallet fees, off-loading, port security and terminal charges, VAT, warehouse storage fees, and cargo insurance extras. Fees vary, and price quotes are based on shipping distance, desired shipping time, order value, volume, and weight. Fees could increase if the shipment is late and delayed cargo charges are added. Once a shipment arrives, inland delivery charges are generally added; therefore, is it important to know if the quoted price includes port-to-port or port-to-door charges.

Customs clearance fees are incurred on orders which arrive by sea or air and must pass through the US Customs and Border Control. A licensed customs broker is required to prepare the necessary documents. Large companies will have an in-house licensed broker, while small to mid-sized companies will outsource this service due to the cost and time required to becoming licensed. The customs broker charges a flat rate based on the volume of imports, but it often has to be adjusted after the delivery is made because the weight, dimensions, and value of the order may not be known prior to shipping.

Duty, also known as tariffs, are taxes imposed on goods produced outside of the home country. The duty is a percent of the total cost and appears as its own line item on the cost sheet. The percentage varies from product category. The US HTS will determine the percentage of duties needed to be paid based on the classification of the product. Once the goods have cleared customs the goods are considered landed. The landed cost is the total cost of goods which includes the freight, duties, and other fees. There are two types of landed costs, LDP and DDP. LDP is the total price of goods up until it reaches the port of destination. DDP is the total price of goods including the delivery to the importers specified destination.

Chapter Review and Discussion

1. What was the primary reason for moving production out of the United States and other developed countries?
2. What roles are involved in global production? Why is understanding of the global supply chain important for costing?
3. What are Incoterms®? Why must we know these universal terms?
4. Most companies in the fashion industry do not request that prices be quoted with the Incoterms® ExW or X-FTY. Why do you think that is?
5. What are the responsibilities of a sourcing agent?
6. What are the different types of fees associated with overseas production?

Activities and Exercises

1. You currently are producing your collection domestically in your home country. However, the cost for producing your apparel line has become too expensive to produce domestically. In addition, you are a smaller company and have a small amount of units to be made with minimal amount of orders. You want to move your production overseas. With this strategy, list out what are the new additional costs you must factor into your pricing in order to maintain a healthy markup and sustain your business. In addition, what are other challenges you may face working with an overseas manufacturer?

2. You are assuming the role of an overseas agent working for a major apparel brand based in New York City. As an agent, you are being paid a commission fee for your services to manage production being done overseas in China. What are some of the basic responsibilities you are required to handle as an agent corresponding with the NYC headquarters? What tasks must you handle in order to meet your production deadlines in the calendar schedule?

Key Terms

CIF (cost, insurance, and freight)
COO (country of origin)
DDP (delivered and duty paid)
direct sourcing
duty
ERP (enterprise resource planning)
ExW (ex-Works)
FAS (free alongside)
FOB (free on board)

freight forwarder
Incoterms®
lab dip
landed
LDP (landed and duty paid)
SKU (stock keeping unit)
sourcing agent
US Harmonized Tariff Schedule (HTS)
X-FTY (Ex-factory)

4 The Factors of Costing

Introduction

To arrive at the cost of a style, the following are considered: fabric, trims, notions, labor, shipping, agent commission, duties, and customs clearance. These components are all found on a cost sheet. However, those elements alone are not the whole picture, and as previously stated, all business expenses must be considered when calculating item costs. As mentioned in Chapter 3, when you produce a product, there are expenses related to production other than the materials, labor, and shipping; those expenses are cost factors of that product. It is important to look at all expenditures as cost factors, and calculate your selling price so each garment sale contributes to covering all these expenses. There are so many more expenses than one realizes when producing garments. No one illustrates that better than Elizabeth Pape, of Elizabethsuzann.com, in her hand-drawn cost-breakdown sketch of her smock-style shirt she shares in her 2017 interview with Racked (Baldwin, 2017). Search online for "Racked, Elizabeth Suzann, money talk" to see the full interview, or follow the QR code here.

As Elizabeth Pape illustrates, there are many places companies spend money other than fabric, trims, or labor, and of which their customers are unaware. There are just so many hidden costs, as shown in her sketch, where the markup must cover all those expenses.

Let's look at all apparel cost factors and expenses. As with the costing of any type of product or service, business costs are categorized as direct, indirect, **fixed**, or **variable**. Now a look at the differences of direct versus indirect and fixed versus variable.

Direct versus Indirect Cost Factors

Direct costs are generally included on a cost sheet. They are specifically involved in the creation and distribution of the item, and there are invoices that connect each to the order. Examples of direct cost factors include direct labor, such as cutting, sewing, and knitting of a style. These activities are priced per minute or hour, or paid by a piece rate. Other direct cost factors include fabric, yarn, trims, notions, shipping, customs clearance, and duty. These are tangible items, services, or expenses that can be listed and tallied.

On the other hand, indirect costs are somewhat questionable in terms of calculating their contribution to the creation and distribution of a style.

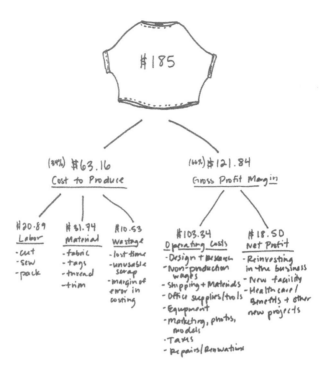

Fig. 4.1 Cost-breakdown sketch by Elizabethsuzann.com's founder, Elizabeth Pape. Elizabeth shows the many costs that must be covered in the garment price.

Indirect costs cannot be traced or linked exactly to any one style. They are related procedures, activities, and expenses that benefit all styles created, and are necessary for the business to operate on a day-to-day basis. Because there are no firm footprints heading directly to the making of a specific style, these factors are usually excluded from cost sheets.

Examples of indirect cost factors include office, manufacturing, and factory overheads such as rent, utilities, equipment purchases and repairs, computers and software, payroll services, accounting and legal fees, and cleaning and office supplies, as well as indirect labor, such as raw materials handling and packing staff, quality assurance staff, receptionists, factory managers, janitorial crew, messengers, and security personnel. Additionally, what is very removed from individual garment style production, but are business expenses nevertheless, include meeting expenses, client lunches or dinners, car services, gifts, travel, hotel and airfare expenses, and marketing, advertising, and trade show costs. These are tracked, of course, but not in relation to specific styles. So are these garment costs, you ask? Yes—just indirectly so.

The amount spent on indirect costs is difficult to calculate. You obviously want to spend as little as possible in these categories so your overhead does not eat into your profit. Nevertheless, a good measure to calculate these expenditures is the **overhead percent**.

To arrive at overhead percent, divide your indirect expenses by direct expenses. Due to the ambiguity of what is an indirect expense, a simple way to calculate those is to first calculate the total costs (i.e., everything spent in a certain time period) and subtract the direct costs spent during that period. The difference is your indirect costs. Yes, everything that remains is your indirect costs.

To quickly determine your indirect costs, subtract the total direct costs from all money that was paid over a certain period of time. What remains is your indirect cost.

Total Costs – Direct Costs = Indirect Costs
$225,000 – $125,000 = $100,000

You then use the difference, which is the indirect costs, to calculate the overhead percent. That equation is: indirect costs divided by total direct costs equal the total overhead percentage.

Indirect Costs ÷ Direct Costs = Overhead Percentage
$100,000 ÷ $125,000 = 0.8
0.8 × 100 = 80%

In this example, the overhead percentage is 80 percent, which means that for everything you sell, 80 percent of the money made must go toward covering your overhead expenses, such as rent, indirect labor, insurance, and so on. That equates to most of your money made. Often a company finds that its overhead costs are greater than the direct costs of goods. Awareness of this percentage allows one to recognize how much must be reduced in order to maintain a high-profit margin.

Of course, to make a greater profit, you should decrease both direct and indirect costs. However, in most cases, a company is unable to enormously lower the direct costs (as that will mean

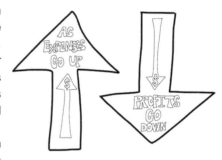

As expenses increase, profits decrease.

using lower quality or less fabric or trims), whereas overhead costs are excellent opportunities to reduce spending, and in turn decrease costs overall and have a more desirable overhead percentage. The lower the overhead percent, the more money a company retains as profit.

It would be more advantageous if the numbers looked like this:

Indirect Costs ÷ Direct Costs = Overhead Percentage
$50,000 ÷ $125,000 = 0.4
0.4 × 100 = 40%

Here the overhead percentage is 40 percent, which means that for every item sold, 40 percent of the money made goes toward covering overhead expenses. 40 percent is more desirable, than 80 percent, as then the remaining 60 percent (instead of a mere 20 percent) are earnings. The lower the overhead percentage, the greater the profit.

Overhead, which includes the indirect costs, can be tracked on a cost-tracking form. You must list and compute the totals of these expenses (either by month, selling season, quarter, or year) to arrive at your total indirect costs, also known as overhead costs.

Overhead Costs Tracking Sheet	
Description	**Total Costs**
Office/showroom space	
Warehouse space	
Material handling	
Equipment/machinery	
Equipment/machinery maintenance	
Office/showroom furnishings	
Office/showroom supplies	
Salaries	
Commissions	
Utilities	
Web services	
Meals/entertainment	
Gifts	
Carfare	
Advertising/marketing	
Shipping costs	
Accounting fees	
Legal fees	
Insurance	
Losses due to theft	
Other	
Grand Total Overhead Costs	

Indirect costs make up the company overhead, and support the business and the products being sold. The expenses are diverse and all-inclusive, so it is easy to miss an expense or two. So it is important to save and file all virtual and physical receipts and invoices. One indirect cost we rarely consider until it occurs is loss. Losses are unexpected expenses that can be due to theft, error, or weather-related damage, such as water, flood, storm, or mildew. If and when loss occurs, it must be accounted for on the cost sheet.

Calculating direct costs is straightforward. We list and add all costs directly on a cost sheets or onto one of two forms: the BOM or the BOL. A **BOM** is a detailed list of all fabric, trims, finding, and other materials that are included in the production of a style, and it lists the supplier name, fiber details, and so on. These components that go onto the BOM can go directly on the cost sheet, but for complex styles that have many fabrics and components, the fabric and all trims and labeling materials are recorded on the BOM. It is also used to keep track of the assortment of materials and packaging for each style, and it is required for each colorway and includes the same materials as the cost sheet.

Table 4.1 Blank bill of materials sheet

Bill of Materials							
Date			**Company**				
Style No.		**Sxs No.**	**Season**				**Group**
Size Range		**Sxs Size**	**Description**				
Material and Description	**Placement**	**Yield or Quantity**	**@ $/yard/ gr/pc**	**Country of Origin**	**Total Cost**	**STYLE SKETCH**	
				GRAND TOTAL COST			

Table 4.2 Bill of materials sheet with list of common raw materials

Bill of Materials						
Date			Company			
Style No.		Sxs No.	Season			Group
Size Range		Sxs Size	Description			
Material and Descrption	Placement	Yield or Quantity	@ $/yard/ gr/pc	Country of Origin	Total Cost	STYLE SKETCH
Fabric						
Lining						
Zippers						
Snaps						
Buttons						
Rivets						
Grommets						
Main Label						
Care Label						
Content Label						
Country of Origin Label						
Size Label						
UPC Tickets						
UPC Stickers						
Joker Tags						
Hangtags						
Tissue Paper						
Poly Bag						
Garment Bag						
Hanger						
Packaging						
Box						
					GRAND TOTAL COST	

Table 4.3 Blank bill of labor sheet

Bill of Labor						
Date			Company			
Style No.		Sxs No.	Season			Group
Size Range		Sxs Size	Description			
Description	Type	Base Rate	SAMs	Total Time	Cost (Time x Rate)	STYLE SKETCH
				TOTAL TIME	TOTAL BOL COST	

Table 4.4 Bill of labor sheet with common labor activities

Bill of Labor Sheet with Common Labor Activities						
Date			Company			
Style No.		Sxs No.	Season			Group
Size Range		Sxs Size	Description			
Description	Type	Base Rate	SAMs	Total Time	Cost (Time x Rate)	STYLE SKETCH
Cutting						
Fusing						
Bundling						
Sewing—Shell						
Sewing—Lining						
Sewing—Other						
Serging						
Seam Finishes—Other						
Topstitch						
Stitching—Other						
Buttons						
Buttonholes						
Notions—Other						
Pressing						
Applique						
Embroidery						
Trim Application						
Hems						
Snipping						
Finishing						
Steaming						
Pressing						
Inspection						
Tagging						
Folding						
Hanging						
Bagging						
Packing						
				TOTAL TIME	TOTAL BOL COST	

The BOM is also a page of the **tech pack** or **technical package.** A tech pack is a detailed set of written and illustrated pages with garment specifications for a style in order for it to be produced. These tech packs are created for every style put into development and is filled out by a person on the design or product development team.

Direct labor activities are often recorded on the **BOL**, where each activity is listed separately by the number of minutes or hours it takes to complete each task. All direct labor activities required to produce a style are listed on the BOL, although not every manufacturer utilizes a BOL, it is a very common practice for large corporate and private-brand manufacturers.

Some businesses input all direct labor activities on their costs sheets. This varies per company.

Fixed versus Variable Costs

Generally, most indirect costs are similar from one month to the next, as they include monthly charges such as rent, insurance, and wages. Just as those costs can eat away at a company's profit, so is the case with *fixed* costs. Fixed costs remain unchanged from month to month and from order to order. Regardless of the unit number total or the total orders produced, fixed costs stay the same. They include office and warehouse rents, payroll, payroll taxes, employee benefits, utilities, administrative costs, insurance, office supplies, company car payments, equipment, and machinery. These are fairly similar to indirect costs. They do not include meals and similar, but otherwise most fixed costs are indirect costs. It is most important to keep fixed costs as low as possible.

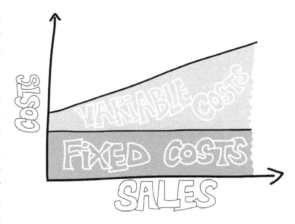

As sales increase (or decrease), the fixed costs remain the same. As sales increase (or decrease), the variable costs increase (or decrease) accordingly.

The reverse of fixed costs is variable costs. Variable costs differ depending on the season and order size, as well as on the complexity of the styles and products being produced. Similar to direct costs, they involve materials and so forth that are used to produce items, and the amounts of those materials and resources change proportionately, and they increase or decrease as the unit quantity of each style and each order increases or decreases. Examples of variable costs include freelance labor and part-time staff, fabric, trims, notions, amount of style detail, shipping, supplies, duty, electricity, inspections, rework services, tariffs, logistics, and so forth.

It is beneficial to list and breakdown both fixed and variable costs so as to keep track and ensure all expenses are being accounted for on the cost sheet and that the price of an item covers all the overhead costs by determining an overhead percentage to be applied to all cost sheets.

For companies just starting out, they should list their expenses on the start-up expense worksheet.

Calculating overhead percentage is one of two ways to ensure all expenses are considered on a cost sheet. The second way is by Activity-Based Costing (ABC) which we explore in Chapter 5. The overhead percentage is easier, but is less activity-specific than ABC.

Table 4.5 Blank bill of materials sheet

ONE TIME START-UP EXPENSES		AMOUNT		NOTES
One Time Start-up Costs:				
Rent Deposit				
Furniture and Fixtures				
Equipment				
Buildout/ Renovations				
Decorating, Painting, and Remodeling				
Installation of Fixtures and Equipment				
Starting Inventory				
Deposits with Public Utilities				
Legal and Other Professional Fees				
License and Permits				
Advertising and Promotion				
Consulting				
Software				
Cash				
Other:				
Other:				
Other:				
Other:				
Total One Time Start-up Costs:				
Monthly Expenses:				
Bank Charges				
Debt Service (Principal & Interest)				
Insurance				
Membership and Dues				
Maintenance and Repairs				
Marketing and Promotion: Advertising				
Marketing and Promotion: Other				
Miscellaneous				
Payroll: Wages (Owner/ Manager)				
Payroll: Wages (Employees)				
Payroll Tax				
Professional Fees: Accounting				
Professional Fees: Legal				
Professional Fees: Other				
Rent				
Subscriptions				
Supplies: Office				
Supplies: Operating				
Telephone				
Utilities				
Other:				
Total Monthly Expenses:				
Number of months required to cover Expenses:				Working Capital
TOTAL START-UP FUNDS REQUIRED:				
Loan Amount (At 80% of Total Start-up)				

Case Study: The Costs of Missing Fabric

Designer Edie Roberts is a successful home fashions designer, and the designer of Edie@Home. Before Edie@Home, Edie co-owned Roberts and Domond, which was a home fashions company. Roberts and Domond started with a vision of offering beautiful high-end soft goods such as placemats, napkins, table runners, throw pillows and more. An early design of theirs was an embroidered silk fabric pillow with corded trim. Edie and her partner were thrilled when they received their first order from ABC Carpet and Home totaling 100 units of the embroidered and corded pillow. As the two partners alone could not produce the pillows by the retailer's requested delivery date, they therefore found a reputable sewing factory in New York City's Chinatown to sew the pillows. The factory manager suggested a cutting room nearby in which the fabric and trim components would be shipped to and cut first. Edie and her partner were delighted they would have their 100 pillows in time and would earn their target markup of 55 percent.

Edie input the wholesale costs of the pillow materials, plus labor and markup percent on to a Roberts and Domond cost sheet. Here are the details:

- Each pillow required 0.5 yards (0.5 m) of the embroidered fabric. The fabric cost $15.00/yard
- Each pillow required 1.75 yards (1.60 m) of the corded trim. The trim cost $3.00/yard
- Each pillow required 1 goose-down pillow insert. Each insert was $5.25
- Each pillow required a 12 inch (30.5 cm) metal zipper. Each zipper cost $0.75
- Each pillow required 1 woven label. Each label: $0.50

Edie ordered the fabric and cording, and arranged to have both shipped to the cutting factory's warehouse. The cutting factory quoted a price of $1.25 per pillow to cut both the fabric and cord.

Edie ordered the zippers and pillow inserts, and had both shipped to the sewing factory's warehouse.

Edie received a sewing and finishing quote from the sewing factory manager of $8.00 per pillow, which included labor and thread.

Edie and her assistant delivered the labels to the sewing factory themselves, and told the factory manager that they'd drive back and pick up the pillows in their own cars as soon as they were completed.

See Table 4.5 for completed production cost sheet.

Over the following ten days, Edie received confirmation that all materials arrived at the cutting and sewing factory locations, and she was advised that production was beginning and the pillows should be ready in four days.

Two days later Edie received a call from the sewing factory manager, who said, "I don't have enough fabric, send more fabric so we can finish the lot." Edie could not understand how they did not have enough fabric. The fabric supplier said they shipped the order complete. This was expensive silk fabric. Edie checked her math again and found she had ordered 50 yards (45.72 m) of the fabric—the correct amount to complete the order. Edie was unsure if the fabric supplier shipped the total yardage. If they did ship it complete, then did it all get delivered to the cutting room warehouse? If it did, was it somehow lost en route between the cutting and sewing factories? Nevertheless, the sewing factory manager insisted she send more fabric so they can finish the production. As she wanted to ensure the pillow order was delivered in time to ABC, Edie had the fabric supplier overnight an additional twenty-five yards to the cutting room warehouse. The overnight shipping charge was $135. Three days later Edie and her partner picked up the pillows, inspected and tagged them at their showroom themselves that night and delivered the pillows on time to the retailer the next day.

What happened to their fabric was a mystery, until a month later Edie has visiting another Chinatown factory and saw what looked just like her beautiful embroidered silk fabric right on the shelf. Edie asked

Table 4.6 Case study: Pillow cost sheet

Basic Production Cost Sheet					
Date 01/20/2000		**Company** Roberts & Domond			
Style No. 105		**Season** Spring 2000			
Size Range 16" by 16"		**Description** Embroidered "Swirly" Pillow			
Fabric Embroidered Silk Fabric					
Fabric	Est. Yield	@Est. $/yard	Est. Cost	Total Est. Cost	**SKETCHES**
Fabric 1: 100% Silk	0.5	$15.00	$7.50		
Fabric 2:					
Freight:			$0.50		
				$8.00	
Trims	Est. Quantity	@Est. $/yard/gr/pc	Est. Cost		
Trim 1: Cording	1.75	$3.00	$5.25		
Trim 2: 12" Metal Zipper	1	$0.75	$0.75		
Trim 3:					
Freight:			$0.25		
				$6.25	
Notions	Est. Quantity	@Est. $/yard/gr/pc	Est. Cost		
Notion 1: Goose-down insert	1	$5.25	$5.25		
Notion 2: Woven label	1	$0.50	$0.50		
Freight:			$1.00		
				$6.75	
Manufacturing	Direct Labor	Contract Work	Contract Work	Est. Cost/Style	
Cutting:			$1.25	$1.25	
Sewing:			$8.00	$8.00	
Finishing:					
Marking/Grading:					
				$9.25	
First Cost of Goods				$30.25	
		Markup Goal %	100%–MU%	Markup $	
		55%	45%	$36.97	
Wholesale Price				$67.22	
		Markup Goal %	100%–MU%	Markup $	
		50%	50%	$67.22	
Retail Price				$134.44	
Manufacturer's Suggested Retail Price (MSRP)				$135.00	

the factory supervisor, "Where did this fabric come from?" The supervisor told her she bought it from a nearby cutting contractor last month with whom she often buys their excess fabric. She checked and told Edie the date she bought it. The date was the very day the fabric has been delivered to the warehouse. Was this error on the part of the cutting contractor? Or was this theft?

Edie, who at that time had over fifteen years experience in the fashion industry, was shocked and frustrated. This contractor error or theft was causing profit loss for the company. She notes today that she learned many costing lessons from that first 100-pillow order. From that point forward, she has revised the figures she inputs on her cost sheets.

Discussion Questions:

- Consider that Edie Roberts purchased 25 additional yards to fulfill the order and had the yardage shipped overnight.
- Calculate the fabric cost per pillow Roberts and Domond spent to complete the order.
- Determine the new total cost of each pillow.
- Calculate the total net profit and wholesale market percentage earned after the partners received payment for the pillow order from ABC.
- What lessons did Edie learn from this first 100-unit order, and what are the possible ways she revised her costing from that point forward?
- Can trust, error, and fraud be a line item on a cost sheet?

If a company fearing a similar situation decided to be present in their factories, how would that effect costing?

Summary

There are many factors involved in costing other than materials, labor, and shipping that are not related to the production of a garment. All business expenses must be considered and are referred to as cost factors. Accounting for all expenditures as cost factors, ensure your selling price will cover all expenses. These costs factors are categorized as direct, indirect, fixed, and variable.

Direct costs are tangible items, services, or expenses that can be listed and tallied. Indirect costs are difficult to calculate as they are the contribution to the creation and distribution of any one style. They are related procedures, activities, and expenses that benefit all styles created, and are necessary for the business to operate. Indirect costs are totaled after a certain period of time and are also known as overhead costs. Indirect costs can also be determined by adding all costs, direct and indirect, and subtracting the direct costs spent during that period of time.

Fixed costs do not vary from month to month or from order to order. A few examples are office and warehouse rents, payroll, utilities, and other costs necessary in running a business. Fixed costs are mostly indirect costs that occur on a regular basis and must be kept as low as possible to not eat away at the profit. Variable costs differ depending on the season and order size, as well as the complexity of the style or product. Similar to direct costs, they involve materials and resources such as freelance labor and part-time staff, fabric trims, shipping, electricity, and so forth. Keeping a list of variable costs is essential in determining an overhead percentage to be applied to all cost sheets.

Activities and Exercises

1. Analyze the below cost factors and compare the overhead percents based on the scenarios.

Table 4.7 Exercise 1 Variable/fixed/direct/indirect costs calculation sheet

	AMOUNT	NOTES
Variable Costs		
Freelance Employee	$25 Per Hour	Cost can change based on skill level and speed of employee.
Seasonal part-time staff	$15 Per Hour	Cost can change based on season jumps in activity.
Fixed Costs		
Warehouse Rent	$3,000 Per Month	Cost will not change month to month.
Payroll	$30,000 Per Month	Cost will not change month to month.
Direct Costs		
Sewing Labor	$3.00 Per Garment	Cost can change if order quantity increases or decreases.
Cutting Labor	$3.00 Per Garment	Cost can change if order quantity increases or decreases.
Indirect Costs		
Visit to Factory	$5,000 One-Time	Cost can change if additional visits are required.
Samples	$20.00 Per Sample	Cost can change if additional samples are needed.

Scenario 1:

A company has decided to add an embroidered pocket to a button-down men's shirt. This will require one freelance employee to work forty hours a week per month, and one seasonal part-time staff to work twenty hours a week per month. They will produce 1,000 of these shirts. The factory which will do the embroidery will be visited once and will send out three samples for approval. What is the overhead cost?

Scenario 2:

After analyzing the costs associated with adding the pocket, the company wants to see how increasing the quantity to 2,000 shirts will impact the overhead cost. What is the overhead cost if the quantity is increased to 2,000 shirts?

2. Take a look in your own closet and pull out two articles of clothing that you bought in your home country. Examine the labels for these garments and find each COO. From there, explain the journey that each product took from the COO and the costs accumulated from when it was shipped to the store from which you bought it in your home country.

3. You are a knits merchant and you have a best-selling style that is being made in Italy. This style was originally considered a fashion style and had only a moderate amount of units produced, as opposed to a massive amount of units planned for a basic style. You need to get this style reordered ASAP, but your factory in Italy cannot deliver in time. What are some other options you can think of in order to get this style reproduced quickly and shipped within two months in order to keep the momentum of sales going?

Key Terms

BOL (bill of labor)	fixed costs
BOM (bill of materials)	overhead percent

5 Activity-Based and Product Development Costing

Activity-Based Costing

Activity-Based Costing (ABC), is a costing method that assigns a monetary value to each and every production activity and overhead expense. It differs from simply calculating your overhead expense as a percentage. ABC places each indirect activity, duty, and cost into categories. In allowing each activity/expense to be categorized, line items have greater precision and accuracy in costing data and management. ABC is complex; it is laborious and can be confusing because it is data- and time-intensive. As opposed to calculating one overreaching overhead percentage, all item types are tracked and costed separately. Many apparel companies feel the collection of all the necessary data is too detail-oriented and time-consuming. Occasionally, those interested in applying ABC start, but then forego the process and go back to a percentage when they experience the level of detail involved in breaking down the cost.

ABC involves breaking down many activities, operations, and duties to the minute, and dividing them by total overhead, administrative, and payroll costs. A true cost is accounted for in ABC as there is fairly full transparency in this methodology. However, as stated, many hesitate to utilize this costing methodology due to the time and labor involved in tracking each activity. They decide that ABC costs more than the value and costing transparency gained. Let's look closer at the details of ABC.

ABC assigns costs to types of manufacturing activities that are traditionally not on a cost sheet, and may or may not be on the Overhead Costs Tracking Sheet. Activities such as material handling, machine set-up for new production batches, and maintaining and repairing equipment are all activities that are included in manufacturing and are often are omitted from the cost sheet. These types of activities are indirect costs, and ABC breaks each down and assigns each a cost by listing the activity types in pooled categories. All expense types are pooled (or grouped), and then each pool is broken down further by specific activity. It is then determined how many times the activity is performed per product, or the number of hours the activity consumes, multiplied by the labor/machine rate to arrive at the cost for each activity in the pool.

If the given ABC breakdown is for a lot of 300 pairs of jeans, then $90 is the material handling expense alone, which means an additional $0.30 is indirectly spent on fabric activities alone to produce the lot of jeans.

Monetary values are calculated not just for material handling but also for each activity and pool, and all of these values can then be added to a cost sheet for a specific style. These activity pools are generally related to manufacturing, and they include material handling, production line setup, equipment maintenance and repair, software and IT, quality control, management and support staff. There are no miscellaneous line items in this costing method.

Chart 5.1 Activity pool calculation example

Activity Pool	Activity	Time (T) in hours	Rate (R) per hour	Cost (T × R)
For Jeans Style KRV-1111				
Material handling	Material receiving	0.75	15.00	11.25
	Material inspection/stocking	1.5	18.00	27.00
	Material handling/pulling	0.75	15.00	11.25
	Material layout	2.25	18.00	40.5
	Total Activity Pool Cost/Style			90.00
	Cost per unit (for 300 units)			**0.30**

ABC costing is often applied when material and direct labor costs have been reduced, but profits are still low. Indirect and overhead costs are often greater than the direct costs of goods, and therefore lower the profit margin. ABC offers a closer look at each category in relation to specific products that are produced. ABC allows a company to dig into the indirect costs, assessing where less obvious cost-cutting can be made. This type of costing can help a company increase its profits. For most companies, ABC costing is applied only on occasion or when needed by certain products due to the detail, time, and labor required.

In ABC, a company can see how much is spent in each pool and decide truly where a large percent of their hidden costs are absorbed. More visibility exists in overhead and indirect costs, and the company can now start chiseling away at the pools that add lost to a product price.

Product Development and Sampling

ABC cost pools generally deal with the manufacturing overhead. However, what is also important, and often overlooked on a cost sheet, is the Product Development (PD) expense. These expenses often occur in another city or country than the production, and when grouped into overhead expenses, the opportunity to see what real impact they have on a product price is lost. The PD team includes designers, merchandisers, product developers, sample hands, and sourcing personnel. These team members are generally well paid, and they often order and purchase many fabric samples, trims, and findings that rarely get allocated to a cost sheet. PD and design teams frequently travel for inspiration, conduct research, source and buy garments, and subscribe to online or physical trend services—not to mention the number of hours they spend creating mood boards, tech packs, and working line sheets. Then there are samples. While most companies attempt to create as few samples as possible to achieve speed-to-market, the sample or samples that are produced are often produced far from the PD team. These samples must be packed and shipped for review and approval, and then fit and corrected, therefore requiring time and workforce and often many international flights to ship the samples to and fro.

PD decisions affect 70 percent of the price of a garment or product, and these important and costly research and development expenses are activities that are generally omitted from cost sheets. When a company tallies their total PD costs and then adds a dollar amount or percent to cover those expenses on each cost sheet, it is known as **Product Development (PD) Loading**. PD Loading is a cushion that helps absorb all that was spent on PD for the style you are costing as well as all the style samples and prototypes that were developed and did not make it to the line.

PD costs are variable costs. Variable costs, as discussed in Chapter 4, are line items that increase or decrease depending upon the season, order size, and complexity of the style. As stated, PD costs are examples of variable costs. They are also examples of indirect costs.

A product developer or designer, no matter how well-seasoned, must be mindful to keep good records from early on in the design and planning processes in order to account for all the development costs and to keep PD costs down. Without appropriate budgeting, it is easy (and quite common) for PD costs to balloon into large figures that eat away at the profit. Each item, from trend research to sourcing and purchasing sample fabrics and trims as well as tech pack work, are included in PD and should be written as a line item on the PD cost-tracking chart. The total PD expenses are divided by the average amount of garments made per year/season. If a company makes on average 300 each of 40 styles, that is 12,000 units/year. If their PD costs total $10,000 on average, then $1.20 should be added to every style to cover PD expenses. If you look back at the traditional cost sheet, you can see product development costs are not there. That said, many companies are beginning to add PD costs, because these costs are high and profits are declining for many. When a company loads PD on to their cost sheet, a large expense, that is not transparent, is now covered.

Estimating Product Development Costs

One challenge designers face when first creating financial worksheets is that most of the costs are guesses or predictions. How many hours does the PD team take emailing and making fabric appointments? How many hours for a particular style are spent writing fitting corrections and uploading photos onto an excel tech pack? No matter how much detail is added to a PD cost-tracking chart, many activities cannot be allocated to one specific style. For example, attending a trend presentation or a trade show seminar where the information gained is utilized for the development and direction of multiple styles and multiple deliveries.

The first time the PD breakdown is tracked, it can be time-consuming. It may seem futile to the new designer to go through the PD costs before starting the process, but without at least looking over all the costs, it is much too easy for spending to get out of control. After the first season, PD costs will be much easier to estimate based on past PD financial-tracking information.

After conducting a preliminary PD cost sheet, it is easier to see where spending can be reined in. For example, costing may be calculated with sampling being done in New York City. After seeing the large costs associated with this, some parts of the PD process may be outsourced. Decisions must be weighed based not just on cost but also on time and quality. Ask any seasoned designer and they will advise you that visiting a factory is a must and that sampling is always done more efficiently if the designer is able to meet the pattern makers and sample sewers in person.

Once again, as mentioned in Chapter 4, all costs must be listed on the cost sheet. Transportation to bring all fabric, trims, and notions to the sample room, as well as any visits you make, is just one aspect to think through when planning PD. Generally, these design, planning, and PD costs are the highest percent of indirect costs on a cost sheet. Below are examples of different line items to be calculated and added to the cost sheet.

Product Development Costs

Research: Primary and secondary research is essential at different levels. Here are different types of research to conduct:

- Trend and color research, media subscriptions
- Mood and trend board creation
- Competitive market research and analysis of points of parity and differentiation in regard to competitors

Trend services and color forecasting: Depending on the size and resources of the company, designers may subscribe and/or have access to trend forecasting companies. WGSN, Peclars Paris, and Fashion Snoops, to name a few, are subscription-based databases filled with mood boards, macro- and micro-trend information, color palette recommendations, flat sketches, and more. These services can run in the thousands of dollars, but have tremendous value. Confirmation that the brand is following industry trends, when using these databases, may mean they have a better chance of meeting the customer's needs.

These subscription fees are a PD cost that must go onto the PD cost-tracking chart.

> Hack: Libraries and colleges have a wealth of information. Instead of hiring a freelance market researcher, try visiting your alma mater or local library to see what trend databases are available. Suggested databases include WGSN, Euromonitor, Peclars Paris, Fashion Snoops, and WWD.

Design: Not all designs are created equally. Each design has different information, and analyzing the overall cost can help make the decision if a style is too costly and therefore should be cut. Considerations for the PD cost-tracking sheet when designing are the following:

- Time spent editing line, cost, lead time, minimums, fit, aesthetics, appropriate, etc.
- Fabric and trimming sourcing, ordering, receiving, logging, and filing of samples.
- Time spent sourcing artwork for prints and patterns, and recoloring them in Photoshop.
- Time logging, commenting, and approving strike-offs, lab-dips, and textile designs.
- Time creating and uploading illustrations and/or CAD sketches for line development.
- Time creating tech packs and detailing fabric, trim, and notion information; how-to-sew/construct illustrations and details; measurement specifications; and packaging requirements.
- Time receiving, commenting, and approving sample garments and construction details.
- Time spent revising design and construction details when a price is too high and a design is being watered down. (e.g., faux pockets or fewer seams can reduce garment price).

Computer-Aided Designers (CAD), Product Developer, and Tech Packs: Depending on the size of the company and budget. CAD sketches and PLM programs may be used. These program expenses must be added to the PD cost sheet.

Sampling is often underestimated and under-recorded when calculating cost. While designs and tech packs are being created, sample fabric and sample trims are being sourced. This sourcing may be done locally by a designer or product developer or be outsourced to an overseas agent or factory. Dyed fabric and trims called lab-dips for color-matching approval, and samples tested and approved for quality, launderability,

Table 5.1 Product development is now loaded on to the traditional cost sheet

Traditional Cost Sheet					
Date		Company			
Style No.	Sxs No.	Season		Group	
Size Range	Sxs Size	Description			
Fabric					
Fabric	Est. Yield	@Est. $/yard	Est. Cost	Total Est. Cost	SKETCHES
Fabric 1:					
Fabric 2:					
Freight:					
Trims	Est. Quantity	@Est. $/yard/gr/pc	Est. Cost		
Trim 1:					
Trim 2:					
Trim 3:					
Freight:					FRONT VIEW
Notions	Est. Quantity	@Est. $/yard/gr/pc	Est. Cost		
Notion 1:					
Notion 2:					
Freight:					
Labor	Direct	Contract Work			
Cutting:					
Sewing:					
Finishing:					
Marking/Grading:					
EST. First Cost of Goods					
Agent Commission %					
Est. Freight					
Duty %					
Clearance %					
Local Freight					BACK VIEW
Product Development					
Total Misc Costs					
Est. LDP / DDP Cost					
Wholesale Markup		Markup Goal %	100% - MU%	Markup $	
Wholesale Price					
Retailer Markup		Markup Goal %	100% - MU%	Markup $	
Retailer Price					
Manufacturer's Suggested Retail Price (MSRP)					

or different properties such as wicking or piling are all activities that can add to development costs. These processes to approve fabrics and trims can often take weeks to complete as comments from designers, sourcing agents, and factory personnel are emailed and updated as fabric and trims are being shipped to and fro. This is completed for all components and for all styles, and due to the length of time it may take, it is quite difficult to assign a cost for these activities, but an estimate is helpful to learn the PD overhead.

Meanwhile, as fabric and trims are being approved, samples must be made simultaneously to achieve the desired fit. Once again this process can take weeks, as all garments must be measured, fit and approved by often both the design and technical teams. The costs associated with garment style and fit sampling adds significant costs to the cost sheet and should be added to the PD cost-tracking chart.

It must also be mentioned that during the sampling process, many samples result in the cancellation of a style. The product may be canceled because of either aesthetics, cost, lack of interest from buyers or any other number of reasons. When styles are cancelled but have been worked on for a considerable amount of time by a PD team, they create costs that are associated with the costs of making others garment styles that have replaced them or remain on the line in their absence.

Lastly, if a company hires freelance or outsourced technical designers, product developers, merchandisers, fit models, or others to oversee these processes, variable freelance staff fees must be entered on to the PD cost-tracking sheet as well.

The listing, calculating, and examining of all PD, planning, and design development costs is eye-opening. These not-so-obvious styles and line development costs are generally the highest indirect cost for a company, and an area prime for expense reduction if product developers and designers can become more mindful of their development decisions. In order to properly record these costs, time is an important factor to be discussed company wide. For example, a designer may list a $2,000 market research trip for the season—calculating this trip affected 500 styles—while a production manager lists a $2,000 factory visit trip, which takes place twice a year. It is unclear by this example how long a season is and how many styles the production manager worked on during the factory visits. PD costing is not a perfect system, but being specific and setting guidelines will give the closest estimates on what has been spent and how to relate it to each garment.

Summary

ABC is a costing method that assigns a monetary value to each and every production activity and overhead expense. This method differs from the more rudimentary method of calculating all overhead as a single percentage, and is utilized under special circumstances where additional time and precision is required for costing.

PD and sampling is a step of the process that is often overlooked in cost sheets, even though the decisions made in PD affect 70 percent of the price of the garment or product. Companies can keep track of their development expenditures in a costing process called PD Loading, which will yield more accurate predictions after the first season adjustment—given the variable nature of the costs.

Research—primary and secondary, and design—on a sketchpad or with CAD software, must be accounted for as well. Similarly, sampling goes on throughout the entire process and often leads to the cancellation of styles of which the company invested money. Variable freelance staff may have even been required to assist with the experimental styles that were cancelled. All these expenditures must be logged.

Most importantly, *time* needs to be openly discussed company wide. You are in the business of fashion, and time-management is key.

Chapter Review and Discussion

1. Why do many companies investigate ABC costing, but then decide to forgo the method?
2. What are the positives and the negatives of ABC?
3. Why do you think PD (and design) costs so often become the largest cost factor of a company's overhead?
4. Why are many companies beginning to load PD expenses on to their cost sheets?
5. If you owned a company and wanted to hire a new position to handle costing, what qualifications would you list in an ad on WWD.com or BOF.com? Write a help wanted ad for an experienced costing manager.
6. Why are some styles cancelled or dropped from a line, and how does that affect costing?

Activities and Exercises

1. List eight—ten duties and activities that a product developer performs that do not go on the traditional cost sheet? Discuss why they do not appear on a cost sheet.

2. Here are sample PD costs. Fill in the total PD costs for one season.

Sample Product Development Costs					
Category	Item	Quantity	Unit*	Price	Total
Research					
	Attend fashion show	1	season*	$2,000	
	Trend service database	1	year	$10,000	
	Freelance market research written trend report	1	month	$3,000	
	Mood boards	1	board	$100	
Design					
	Tech packs	1	month	$1,000	
	Trim and fabric approval	1	month	$1,000	
	Fit comments	1	month	$1,500	
	Design comments	1	month	$500	
Sampling					
	Domestic sampling	1	sample	$100	
	Store bought samples	1	sample	$20	
	Travel to factory	2	year	$5,000	

* 3 months in a season

3. Using the given chart, what is the estimated PD cost if 2,000 styles were created? And, what is the estimated PD cost if 900 styles were created? Or if 4,000 styles were created? As seen, the PD and design teams use many resources for research, inspiration, and sourcing. How does this affect their product costs in terms of quantity and assortment?

Key Terms

ABC (activity-based costing)	product development loading

6 Target Market and Private-Label Pricing

Thinking through the line as a whole is just as important as analyzing individual style costs. When planning a line, a few strategic questions must be considered in order to work toward profitability. Is there a good mix of **staple** and **fashion** pieces? What is the price range of the line? How many colors are offered throughout the line? Are too many fabrications driving up the cost? There are countless questions to be asked and answered, which can help reduce unnecessary spending. All of these questions cannot be answered until the customer you are targeting is identified, and the most strategic question of all can be asked: Does the price range work for the selected target market? Let's explore how the target market affects the cost and retail price of a garment.

Identifying Your Target Customer

Before selecting a pricing strategy it is important to identify the target customer. A target market or target customer is who you have in mind when you develop the item. The target customer is who you envision using or wearing your product, and your ultimate goal is for this group to purchase, use, and wear the item.

To begin, the market (or customer group) must be researched in terms of income level, age range, beliefs, attitudes, shopping behavior and geographical locations. Then a line, product, and promotion is created to attract said group(s).

Why is knowing your customer important when costing a product? This is because you must decide how much your intended customer will pay for your products, and then source and select materials, factories and processes that will cost out at the price this customer will pay. How much our customer is willing to pay depends on their age, income level, and how and where they shop. Customers are identified by **demographics**, **psychographics**, and/or **geographics**. These factors assist in creating a product at the price that a target customer is willing to pay. Therefore, gathering information regarding your target customers' purchasing habits helps narrow the pricing strategy selected. Example questions:

- Where do my target customers shop?
- How much will they pay for different product offerings?
- What are their quality expectations?

It is important to note that demographics, psychographics, and geographic information will only tell part of the story. A customer may be a bargain shopper for fashion or trend items, but pay a higher price for handbags, shoes, or services. Surveying potential customers can help answer some of these unknowns and allow you to know the intangible value your target customer places on various items.

Types of Pricing

There are different pricing strategies used by different brands depending on their target market and brand values. A product's selling price must be consistent with a company's image. A designer price point brand exudes luxury and status, therefore the customer's pricing expectation is quite high. Many companies accomplish a consistent price range of products and branding to go along with that pricing by describing their price strategy in their slogans. For example, Walmart's slogan for nineteen years, "Always Low Pricing," and now their current slogan, "Save Money. Live Better," tells us that their customer is price sensitive and looking for deals (Mui and Rosenwald 2008). Search online for "Huffington Post, Walmart slogan", or follow the QR code for the full article . Gucci provides a perfect example with their slogan, "Quality is remembered long after price is forgotten." It is clear that their pricing strategy is focused on meeting the needs of the luxury customer. Before diving into different pricing strategies, let's explore the relationship between price and **value**. Value is the relationship between price and quality. A customer is willing to accept the low quality of a fast fashion item because the price is also low. A customer is willing to pay a very high price for a luxury bag because the expectation is this bag is an investment piece or will last them a lifetime. High-end designer items have a high value in the mind of the customer.

Let's take a closer look at the pricing strategies given here.

Status pricing or **premium pricing** is used to target a more affluent or aspirational customer. As previously mentioned, retail price often equates to quality in the mind of the customer; therefore, a certain price must be used in order to compete in the luxury market. Status/premium pricing includes all the direct costs traditionally on a cost sheet, as well as a large overhead percent to cover the high rents for the shops and the often expensively produced marketing and ad campaigns. Status-priced brands include Burberry, Gucci, and Prada to name a few. The brands that use this pricing strategy do not sell large quantities of most items, as these are aspirational products for most shoppers. Brands and retailers that use this strategy add a large markup to their costs to cover their often-prestigious location rents and high-end marketing campaigns.

Penetration pricing, typically seen with a new product attempting to take away significant market share from its competitors, sets the price lower than the competitor, with the hopes it will make up the price difference with a high sales volume. Penetration pricing includes all the direct costs traditionally on a cost sheet, with a much lower markup percent added to the total cost. The penetration pricing strategy has been utilized by Target, Amazon, and Walmart. It is important to note that many of these retailers will begin with penetration pricing but slowly move to another pricing strategy once the customer accepts the retailer as always having the lowest prices. The retailer slowly increases prices and receives a greater profit without the customer noticing.

Competitive/market pricing is used by brands that price their goods quite close to, and in the same price range, as the other similar retailers and brands in the marketplace. They use other similar selling items as a benchmark, and price their products in this range. This pricing strategy allows companies to compete by product, not price, and it is an often-used strategy when entering markets fairly saturated with similar products (jeans for instance). Brands may use this strategy for specific products within its line. For example, Levi's uses competitive pricing for their classic 501 jeans, but for new trend items may adopt a high-low strategy (see further). The brands that use competitive or market pricing generally apply a just-above keystone markup.

High-low pricing, commonly used in department stores, sets a high price and slowly discounts over the course of days, weeks, and months. This strategy works because customers have been conditioned to purchase on sale. Buying items on sales give the customer a sense of "winning." If an item is 50 percent off, customers believe they are getting a great deal, but the high-low pricing strategy is geared to give customers this false sense of satisfaction. Department stores typically reduce prices seventeen—nineteen days after an item is first put on the selling floor. An additional discount will be added as the merchandise makes its way to the sales rack. Retailers will build in this discount to their cost sheets and will still receive a profit even when the garment reaches 75 percent off.

Everyday low pricing (EDLP), a strategy perfected by Walmart, is the opposite of high-low pricing. Instead of playing the "sales game," retailers give the lowest price, but of course still receive a profit. The retailer is banking on the notion that a large percent of customers will purchase, and that many will buy large quantities of the item. They may not make a large profit by selling an individual item, but they make a very healthy profit off of the large quantity sold. This strategy builds customer loyalty and gives the perception that the customer does not need to do research because the retailer is always offering the lowest price. For example, Walmart will offer the lowest price of all its competitors for toilet paper, which will be featured in the retailer's circular newspaper coupon, but have slightly higher prices on milk. Walmart is betting that a customer does not want to make multiple trips to different retailers and will accept the higher price for some items.

Competitor Research

Many factors must be taken into account when selecting a pricing strategy: **price range** and **price point**. Analyzing competitor pricing is essential to remaining competitive. Collecting a list of five to ten competitors and placing them on a **perception map**, a tool to identify customers' perception of different brands, is one way to identify the **white space** in the market in relation to price and quality.

Fig. 6.1 **Perception map of popular brands.**

Table 6.1 Example of an in-work cost sheet with edits and revisions

Production Cost Sheet					
Date 03/2021		**Company** KRV Designs			
Style No. 1000	**Sxs No.** 200	**Season** Spring Delivery 1		**Group** Women's Victorian Tops	
Size Range XS–XL	**Sxs Size** M	**Description** Flounce Front Long Sleeve Button Down Shirt			
Fabric 14 mm Silk CDC					

Fabric	Yield/ Style	Cost/ Yard	Cost/ Garment	Total/ Garment	**SKETCHES**
Fabric 1: Silk CDC	~~1.5~~ 1.3	~~$6.98~~ $6.41	~~$10.47~~ $8.33		
Lining: Interfacing	~~0.2~~ .15	~~$1.99~~ $1.89	~~$0.40~~ $0.28		
				$8.62	

Trims	Yield/ Style	Cost/ Yard/ Gr/Pc	Cost/ Garment	Total/ Garment	
Trim 1: 18L Buttons at CF	8	$0.01	$0.08		
Trim 2: 14L Buttons at Cuff	4 — 2	$0.01	~~$0.05~~ $0.02		
				$0.09	

Notions	Yield/ Style	Cost/ Yard/ Gr/Pc	Cost/ Garment	Total/ Garment	
Notion 1: Thread	26	$8.00	$0.21		
Notion 2: Labels	1	~~$0.50~~ $0.48	$0.48		
Notion 3: Hanger	1	$0.75	$0.75		
Freight: Vendor > Factory				$1.44	

Labor	Country	Direct Labor	Contract Work	Total/ Garment	
Cutting	China	~~$1.55~~ $1.45			
Sewing	China	~~$4.95~~ $4.55			
Finishing		$0.40			
Marking/Grading		$0.75			
				$7.15	

Cost of Goods				$17.30	
Agent Commission %	5%	$0.87			
Freight		~~$1.00~~ $0.55			
Duty %	7%	$1.21			
Clearance %	2.5%	$0.43			
Local Freight		~~$1.00~~ $0.35			
LDP / DDP Cost				$20.71	

	A	B	C	D	
Sell Price	$38.00	$42.00	$44.00	$46.00	**BACK VIEW**
Net Profit (Sell Price less Cost)	$17.29	$21.29	$23.29	$25.29	
Net Profit % (Net Profit div by Sell)	45.50%	50.69%	52.93%	54.98%	

FRONT VIEW

Target Market Costing

Now that we have analyzed different pricing strategies, how do we identify your target customers' price needs, and what strategy your competitors are using? Let's dig into how to fill in and adjust your cost sheet. Costing sheets are working documents. Starting top down, all items are filled in from materials, labor, direct and indirect costs. The figures should be analyzed and adjusted, bottom-up, if the cost becomes too high. Depending on the markup added for wholesale and/or retail, the final price might be too high for the target market pricing. Looking back through the cost factors, there are places cost can be cut or reduced. Going line by line, the production manager, product developer, designer, or costing manager can decide to reduce the number of seams in a garment, change the type of fabric used to a lighter-weight or less-expensive quality, or decide to move production to a cheaper country or factory as just a few examples of ways and places to cut costs. These changes should be taken into consideration while keeping in mind what stage of development the product is in at the moment. It is quite common to sit in costing meetings looking at samples, with costs sheets in hand, and simply cross-out and make edits directly to a cost sheet. Costing targets drive style changes (more on this in Chapter 8).

Of course, it might be too late to make too many changes to a cost sheet if bulk production fabric is purchased or if orders have been placed. For these reasons, it is essential to comb through cost sheets during pre-production costing, which is early in the development stage.

Value-Based versus Cost-Based Pricing

Keeping in mind one's target customer and pricing strategy relates to a target retail prices, it is important to remember that the target retail price correlates to cost. Depending on whether the product is labeled with an established brand name or an unknown designer will determine the retail price customers will accept. A well-known brand could potentially keep costs low while adding a significant mark-up. This brand would use **value-based pricing**. Value-based pricing is when the desired retail price is first identified, and then one works backward from that price to determine what the product should cost.

Value-Based Costing			
Customer accepts price as great value & knows how much will they pay >	Retail price >	Mark up % >	Cost

On the flip side is **cost-based pricing**, where one starts with the actual costs of the product and then works forward adding markup from those costs to arrive at a retail selling price, which hopefully appeals to the customer.

Cost-Based Costing			
You calculate the cost to make the product >	Mark up % >	Retail price >	Customer

An unknown designer who is competing with established brands may set a goal to offer a price just below their competitor. In that case, they will use value-based pricing.

When a company does choose value-based pricing, they work backwards from a selling price their customer finds valuable. They must determine the target cost of materials and source accordingly. Nine times out of ten, fabric is the largest direct cost factor. A good rule of thumb in determining material costs from a retail selling price is to divide by eight. This is because, generally in fashion, the fabric cost for a garment is roughly one-eighth of the retail price if there was a wholesaler involved. Labor, trim, plus production services are generally another one-eighth.

For a wholesale brand, who knows the price they wish to sell at retail, they can use value-based costing and calculate the target fabric costs by working backwards from the desired retail price. For instance, a manufacturer/designer has a new children's swimwear design. They look online and visit stores to research other children's swimwear lines their target customer purchases. They find similar-type swimsuits selling on average at $40.00 retail. As the same end-customer is being targeted, and the customer finds value in this price, they should be in roughly the same price range to be competitive. Therefore they must also produce with similar cost factors to achieve that retail selling price.

To determine what that other manufacturers paid for fabric and trim in order to sell the swimsuit at $40.00 retail, work backwards—first to the wholesale cost. Assuming a slight higher-than-keystone markup was used, we determine the wholesale price

$$R \times (100 - MU\%) = \text{Wholesale price (W/S)}$$
$$\text{Given: Retail price} = \$40.00 \text{ and } MU = 52\%$$
$$\$40.00 \times (100\% - 52\%) = W/S$$
$$40.00 \times 0.48 = \$19.20$$

We can assume that the online store or physical retailer purchased the $40.00 swimsuit from the branded manufacturer for approximately $19.20 per piece.

For a manufacturer to sell a garment to a retailer at approximately $19.00, they must get it produced for roughly half that price, as often a keystone is used.

$$W/S \text{ price} \times (100\% - MU\%) = \text{First Cost (FC)}$$
$$\text{Given: Wholesale price} = \$19.20 \text{ and } MU = 50\%$$
$$\$19.20 \times (100\% - 50\%) = FC$$
$$19.2 \times 0.50 = \$9.60$$

Therefore, the other swimsuit manufacturers paid approximately $9.60 (or $9.00 to $10.50) in FCs to sell the swimsuit at $19.20 wholesale.

The $9.60 FC per piece includes fabric cost, trimming costs, and production labor costs. Generally, materials are half or a tad more than half of the FC. In this case, FC equals $9.60, therefore we can estimate that the fabric and trims used in a $40.00 swimsuit at retail equal $4.80 to $5.00 per swimsuit.

The shortcut of dividing a retail price by eight to arrive at a materials cost estimate brings us to the same answer

$$\$40.00 \div 8 = \$5.00$$

Upon knowing the price you hope a garment will sell at retail, you can work backward and figure out what you need to pay in total material costs for a similar garment. This information helps you source your materials in the best price range for your target selling price.

If a mill tells you their swimsuit fabric is $4.00 per yard and you need 0.5 yards (0.45 m) per piece, then that is $2.00 per garment and you can safely guess that the quality will not be what the customer will find valuable. And if a mill advises a price per yard of $16.00 for a certain swimwear fabric, then you will want to source from another mill, as $8.00 of fabric per swimsuit will be too high in fabric costs. If you know you must pay $4.80–$5.00 in total materials costs per style, you can assume your fabric should be $3.50–$4.00 per piece and your trims $1.00–$1.50 per piece.

Every brand must make tough sourcing and production choices to balance cost, quality, and perceived value. Brands must keep their target customer in mind, and their target selling prices must cover their direct and indirect expenses and overhead cost, and must ensure enough markup is added to cover any unknown costs that may occur during the production and distribution processes.

Private-Label Pricing

When retailers sell merchandise with their own retail name or exclusive brand on the label, it is known as **private label**. Private label merchandise appears in two ways: one is when a large retailer, such as a department store or specialty chain, develops an exclusive line to sell in their stores alongside other wholesale/proprietary brands (such as Style & Co. at Macy's). Two is when a private-brand retailer develops its own exclusive and extensive collection to sell in their stores under their retail-store name (such as Zara or Gap). In producing private label merchandise, a retailer applies a higher markup percent, as there is no wholesaler or middle company's profit that must also be paid.

As discussed in Chapter 2, the basic keystone markup is applied by both wholesaler and retailer

First Cost × 2 = Wholesale Price   **Wholesale Price × 2 = Retail Price**
$10.00 × 2 = $20.00 $20.00 × 2 = $40.00

When a retailer creates their own private label line, whether they work directly with a factory or have a proprietary-brand manufacturer produce the line, the two markup phases are reduced to one. The retailer is able to apply one greater markup percent, and the wholesale markup is eliminated. The retailer applies and earns a greater profit, and the customer gets a sharper price.

In traditional wholesale pricing, if an item has a $12.00 landed cost, and is keystoned first to wholesale, then also the keystone markup is applied to achieve a retail price. The selling price is $48.00. The retailer has a 50 percent markup and earns $12.00 for each full-price sale.

(Retail Price − Wholesale Price) ÷ Retail Price = Markup
($48.00 − $24.00) ÷ $48.00 = Markup
$24.00 ÷ $48.00 = 0.5
0.5 × 100 = 50%

Using the markup percent formula, we also see the style has a total markup of 75 percent between the two phases.

(Retail Price − Landed Cost) ÷ Retail Price = Markup
($48.00 − $12.00) ÷ $48.00 = Markup
$36.00 ÷ $48.00 = 0.75
0.75 × 100 = 75%

In private-label manufacturing and private-label pricing, the retailer, who is the designer and product developer, omits the name-brand wholesale markup and increases the total markup. The same style with a $12.00 landed cost as private label can sell at retail at $42.00 and earn the retailer $30 for each full-price sale, and increase the markup from 50 percent to 66 percent.

(Retail Price − Landed Cost) ÷ Retail Price = Markup
($44.00 − $12.00) ÷ $48.00 = Markup
$32.00 ÷ $48.00 = 0.66
0.66 × 100 = 66%

This is a 16 percent increase in revenue per item sold for the retailer, and this more competitive, greater profit margin illustrates why private label goods have greatly increased in past years.

See the sample private-label cost sheet. The cost sheet for private label is identical to the traditional cost sheet, with the exception of the markup line items. As there is no wholesale price, the markup to retail is added directly to the LDP or DDP cost. The markup is variable, but averages 55 percent to 85 percent depending on the style and quantity.

Private-Label Pricing Has a Competitive Advantage

The private label retailer marks up the goods from cost to retail at a greater markup rate but must keep in mind that their competition includes well-known (advertised) brands. Not only can private-label retailers provide slightly lower pricing because of the lower cost from the branded competitors but they are also

Table 6.2 The private label cost sheet has only one line for adding markup, as there is no middle party

Private Label Retailer Cost Sheet					
Date		Company			
Style No.	Sxs No.	Season			Group
Size Range	Sxs Size	Description			
Fabric					
Fabric	Est. Yield	@Est. $/yard	Est. Cost	Total Est. Cost	SKETCHES
Fabric 1:					
Fabric 2:					
Freight:					
Trims	Est. Quantity	@Est. $/ yard/gr/pc	Est. Cost		
Trim 1:					
Trim 2:					
Trim 3:					
Freight:					FRONT VIEW
Notions	Est. Quantity	@Est. $/ yard/gr/pc	Est. Cost		
Notion 1:					
Notion 2:					
Freight:					
Labor	Direct	Contract Work			
Cutting:					
Sewing:					
Finishing:					
Marking/Grading:					
EST. First Cost of Goods					
Agent Commission %					
Est. Freight					
Duty %					
Clearance %					BACK VIEW
Local Freight					
Product Development Costs					
Total Misc Costs					
Est. LDP / DDP Cost					
Private Label Retailer Markup		Markup Goal %	100%–MU%	Markup $	
Private Label Retailer Price					
Manufacturer's Suggested Retail Price (MSRP)					

advised to do so in order to retain a competitive advantage. This is especially true for retailers, such as department stores, which sell the branded product within the same space as their private label. This direct competition can benefit or pose as a challenge to the private label. Imagine seeing a Ralph Lauren women's polo shirt for $89.50 at Macy's. Macy's private label, Charter Club, is able to sell a similar polo shirt for $39.50. The customer may have entered the store after seeing Ralph Lauren's advertisements, but ends up leaving with the Charter Club polo due to its lower price and similar quality. With an average of 70 percent, private label is certainly a very profitable business model.

For private label, or direct-to-consumer selling, the calculations for value-based pricing differ slightly. In these cases, the fabric is roughly one-sixth of the retail selling price. A private-brand company again works backwards from the target retail price.

For instance, if the earlier example of children's swimwear is private label, then instead of selling at $40.00, it may sell at approx. $30–$34. FC is still $9.60, and fabric must still cost roughly $4.80–$5.00 per swimsuit. The private label maker adds a higher markup, but the fabric cost (when utilizing value-based pricing) is one-sixth, instead of one-eighth of retail.

$$\$32.00 \div 6 = \$5.33$$

The pricing may be $8.00 lower for a similar swimsuit, made with equal-quality fabric and workmanship, but the private-label profit is greater, as when the swimsuit was sold to the retailer from the wholesaler, the wholesaler applied a 50 percent markup, and the retailer applied a 52 percent markup.

$$FC \div (100 - MU) \times 100 = W/S \ and \ W/S \div (100 - MU) \times 100 = R\$$$
Wholesaler adds 50 percent markup *and* Retailer adds 52 percent markup

$$\$9.60 \div (100 - 50) \times 100 = \$19.20 \ and \ \$19.20 \div (100 - 52) \times 100 = \$40.00$$
$$\$9.60 \div 50 \times 100 = \$19.20 \ and \ \$19.20 \div 48 \times 100 = \$40.00$$

Compared to the private-label swimsuit that skips the middle person and applies a 70 percent markup to sell a considerably lower-priced piece of swimwear:

$$FC \div (100 - MU) \times 100 = P/L \ \$$$
The private-label retailer adds 70 percent markup

$$\$9.60 \div (100 - 70) \times 100 = \$32.00$$
$$\$9.60 \div 30 \times 100 = \$32.00$$

After this explanation of value-based pricing, it must be stated that it is quite difficult to make a profit if you use value-based pricing. Yes, you may be creating a style that the customer perceives has a good price; however, if you do not work cost-forward, then you may not cover all your indirect expenses. The benefit of cost-based pricing is that you ensure all costs are met.

Summary

Before pricing can begin, a company needs to identify their target market/customer. Where does my target customer shop? How much would my target customer spend on a hoodie or a handbag? What are their quality expectations? Answering these questions will allow a company to know how much they can spend and charge for their products.

Status pricing or premium pricing is used to target a more affluent or aspirational customer. Brands and retailers that use this strategy add a large markup to their costs to cover their often-prestigious location rents and high-end marketing campaigns.

Penetration pricing is typically seen with a new product attempting to take away significant market share from its competitors, and it sets the price lower than the competitor with the hopes it will make up the price difference with a high sales volume.

Competitive/market pricing is used by brands that price their goods quite close to, and in the same price range, as the other similar retailers and brands in the marketplace.

High-low pricing is commonly used in department stores, and it sets a high price and slowly discounts over the course of days, weeks, and months.

EDLP is a strategy perfected by Walmart, and it is the opposite of high-low pricing. Instead of playing the "sales game," retailers give the lowest price, but of course still receive a profit.

Value-based pricing is when the desired retail price is first identified, and then one works backward from that price to determine what the product should cost. Cost-based pricing is where one starts with the actual costs of the product and then works forward adding markup from those costs to arrive at a retail selling price. Brands must keep their target customer in mind, and their target selling prices must cover their direct and indirect expenses and their overhead cost and ensure enough markup is added to cover any unknown costs that may occur during the production and distribution processes.

Private label occurs when a retailer decides to sell merchandise with their own retail or exclusive name on the label, therefore, skipping over the middleman, that is, the wholesaler. There are two types of private label: department or specialty store and private-brand retailer. These two retailers can create their private label line by working directly with a factory or a proprietary-brand manufacturer. Private label results in two markup phases being reduced to one, allowing a 70 percent markup. Although the cost of goods is the same, private label allows a private-brand retailer to add a greater markup, offer a lower pricing, and earn a larger profit.

Chapter Review and Discussion

1. How do you identify target customers? What questions should you ask and what information do you need? Why is it important, in costing, to truly know who your target customer is?
2. What are the five pricing strategies? How are they each they different? Do you feel a fashion brand can stick with one pricing strategy throughout the lifetime of the brand?
3. Why is knowledge of pricing strategies important to a costing professional?
4. Why do some retailers decide to create their own private label lines? Why is this model thought to be so profitable? How are the markup opportunities different?
5. What are your three favorite fashion brands? Which pricing strategy do you think that they each utilize?
6. What is the difference between value-based and cost-based pricing? What are the risks and benefits to each?

Activities and Exercises

1. Pair up with a classmate and each select and download five retailers/brands. Look up and download each of their logos and slogans. Have your classmate identify each of the five brands' pricing strategies and estimate their mark-up ranges.

2. If you are designing an outerwear line, you may want to price yourself in the same range as benchmark brands that have similar target customers. You look online at several department stores and you see similar category coat styles ranging from $145–$195, with an average price of $170.00. Define your company and determine how much the cost of your fabric should be.

3. Create a pricing strategy board online or on Pinterest. Label each area with the different pricing strategies and add photos from at least three to four fashion brands that price their lines in each of the strategies.

Key Terms

competitive pricing	price point
demographics	price range
everyday low pricing	private label
fashion	staple
high-low pricing	status pricing
penetration pricing	value
perception map	value-based costing
premium pricing	white space

7 Margins, Markups, and Markdowns

Profitability is the goal of every company. Finding the right profit margin is as essential as finding the right fit of the garment or the right customer for your product. Consistent growth can only be achieved through profitability. The pressure for companies to grow from shareholders results in a high stakes game of chasing low labor costs, diversification of product offerings, as well as the need to expand into new markets. Well in advance of the delivery date to the customer, companies must plan their future product lines with past financial performance as their main source of forecasting projections. There is no sure-fire way for companies to ensure profitability. For new businesses, profitability typically takes a few years to accomplish, as joining the already-saturated apparel marketplace and competing with established brands is no easy feat. But it can be done, and profitability leads to success and the ability for the company to continue.

Profit Margins

Profit margins differ from markups because they measure profit in separate ways. Markup, as discussed throughout the book, is added to COGS. Markup is the difference (in dollars or percentage) between the costs and the selling price, whereas margin is what remains after you sell an item. Margin is the difference (in dollars or percentage) between the selling price and the profit.

   If your cost of goods is $7.50 and you sell a headband for $12.50, then your profit is $5.00 per piece. To calculate your margin after the headband has been sold, you divide your profit amount by the retail selling price.

Retail $ – Cost ÷ Retail $ = Margin
$12.50 – $7.50 ÷ $12.50 = Margin
$5.00 ÷ $12.50 = 0.4
0.4 = 40% Margin

With a $7.50 COGS and a headband selling price of $12.50, a 40 percent margin is made. This means the company keeps 40 percent of each headband sold.

   A 40 percent margin equates to a higher starting markup. Markups are always higher than margins, because margin looks at how much is left, after paying for all costs and expenses, while markups look at what has been added to the cost. The above 40 percent margin equates to a much higher markup.

$$\text{Retail \$} - \text{Cost} \div \text{Cost} = \text{Markup}$$
$$\$12.50 - \$7.50 \div \$7.50 = \text{Markup}$$
$$\$5.00 \div \$7.50 = 0.666$$
$$0.666 = 67\% \text{ Margin}$$

As demonstrated, a 66 percent markup equals a 40 percent margin. A markup is always a higher percentage than the margin. Here are common markups and their corresponding margins:

Markups vs. Margins	
Markup %	Margin %
20	17
25	20
30	23
40	29
50	33
60	38
75	43
100	50

What is very important to understand is that when you know the margin, you need to make you can add a corresponding target markup to meet that goal.

When selecting profit margin and markup percentages, they must be numbers that will sustain the business and allow it to grow. Profit markups typically range from 25 percent to 75 percent or higher, depending on the chosen pricing strategy (see Chapter 6). Companies do not choose one definitive markup percentage to add to every style. Each product requires its own markup/margin. This depends on the customer, quantity, retail distribution, as well as if the product is a fashion or staple item. It is acceptable for profit margins to vary per product, as long as the markup percentage added to each individual style averages out high enough to maintain a healthy profit. Generally, companies add a higher profit markup to styles that will receive lesser distribution and a lower profit percentage to styles that are produced in large quantities or are selling in many retailers and distribution points.

It is not always as simple as illustrated in Chart 7.1, as many external factors can affect target profit margins. Retailers like Amazon and Walmart with massive influence, footprints, and product lines are driving down retail prices, and therefore profits. Profit margins must account for all cost factors, direct and indirect, as well as healthy padding in order to grow the business. Markdowns, promotional discounts, and coupons must also be accounted for, and will be discussed in greater detail later in the chapter.

Finding the right profit margin may take a few seasons if you are just starting out. Many businesses begin by applying a keystone, or slightly higher, markup and adjusting with each product or season. The difference of 1–2 percent, or a few dollars or cents makes all the difference in having a sustainable profit, a bestseller, or the unfortunate need to severely discount an item. Ultimately, the goal is to add a markup to your cost of goods and expenses, and achieve a profit margin that will sustain your business. Too great a markup and you may price yourself out of the market. Too low a margin and you may not cover all your expenses. Where and how you are selling must be taken into consideration. If you cannot achieve your desired profit percentage, then you must raise your selling price (generally not a winning strategy) or go back and attempt to reduce your costs (see Chapter 8 on reducing costs).

Chart 7.1 Example of how margins can differ depending on style classification

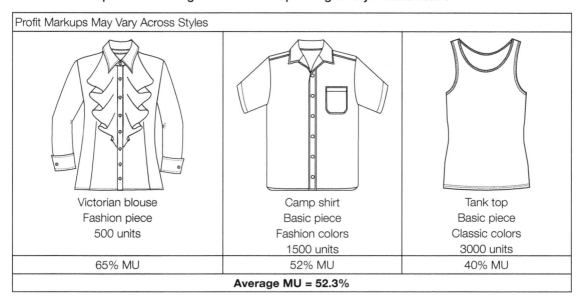

Profit Markups May Vary Across Styles		
Victorian blouse Fashion piece 500 units	Camp shirt Basic piece Fashion colors 1500 units	Tank top Basic piece Classic colors 3000 units
65% MU	52% MU	40% MU
Average MU = 52.3%		

Omni-Channel Retailing

Not too long ago, retailers fit into only one category of sales, but with **omni-channel** distribution most retailers now participate in a variety of retail formats. These various types of retail formats result in from the need for different profit margins. For example, Ralph Lauren's quintessential polo shirt is sold at the Ralph Lauren flagship store, Polo Ralph Lauren, online on the Ralph Lauren website, Ralph Lauren outlets, and at Macy's as well as at Macy's discount stores. All of these polo shirts are not of the same quality, therefore, they are

The end price can vary slightly depending on the type and scale of the retail establishment.

not costed and marked up the same way. This example does not even include all the sub-brands under Ralph Lauren.

As discussed previously, wholesale and private label costing have different financial implications. Large brands, such as Ralph Lauren mentioned earlier, often find themselves competing not only with their private label competitors but also with themselves. Brands used to have the power of setting retail prices; however, with the advent of the internet and the democratization of information, that power is now firmly placed in the hands of the customer. As Amazon has gained momentum and market share, they now demand Ralph Lauren meet their MSRP. Amazon sets a retail price of $33.98, forcing Ralph Lauren to work with manufacturers to revise materials, construction, and price. Working backward with a 50 percent markup, Ralph Lauren sets a price of $16.99, and their cost would be approximately $8.50 per shirt.

Ralph Lauren obviously has great pull and relationships throughout the industry with a variety of retailers. For the new designer this is not the case. In order for new and upcoming designers and clothing lines to develop a relationship with a large retailer, consignment is often the only selling term available. Retailers will accept a new product with the caveat that the product will be placed in a limited amount of stores, with no upfront payment. This means that the designer must pay for all COGs, direct and indirect costs, shipping, and so on and deliver the goods with no guarantee of payment. The terms may be set for sixty or ninety days where any product not sold can be returned to the designer. This puts a significant financial risk on a new company, as the selling and profit margin is uncertain. Therefore, when consigning, the profit margin percent should be increased to cover the fact that some pieces may quite likely be returned.

In response to the Amazons, Walmarts, Ralph Laurens, and consignment trends, there are efforts to regain control over pricing and profitability. These efforts include new designer brands and large national brands going directly to the consumer. The direct-to-consumer model cuts the middle man, the large retailer, resulting in higher profits for the brand as well as the ability to set retail prices just below branded competitors, thus giving a competitive advantage. The typical direct-to-consumer markup averages at 60 percent. With e-commerce, brands can sell a product without the significant cost of retail space, sales assistants, insurance, and many other costs. However, other costs are incurred in order to hold merchandise, distribute accordingly, and provide online assistance. New designers can also participate in **pop-up** events, **shop-in-shops**, and **drop shipping**, as well as e-commerce.

This multi-channel retail strategy where low prices and big sales are driving the excitement has created a marketplace where costing and pricing needs to be extremely sharp. Costing in today's marketplace requires strategic planning and forethought in order to maximize profits and minimize losses. Although much of this chapter thus far discusses making profit, sadly, the desired profit margin is not always achieved and therefore profit earned is greatly reduced. This is loss. Profit loss can be incurred through discounts, markdowns, and chargebacks. As mentioned earlier in this chapter, US customers have been conditioned to look for sales when shopping. These markdowns eat away at the profit margin, causing retailers to inflate profit margins so they can reduce the prices to meet customer expectations. Each retailer must choose their pricing strategy based on their target market needs and must stick to the plan to avoid confusion. Now, we will examine the three types of profit loss and how they affect the retailers, wholesaler, and manufacturer.

Discounts

Discounts are planned losses. This may seem contradictory to a retailer's overall mission to gain profitability, but as mentioned certain markets and retail settings demand discounted merchandise sales in order to move product. Discounts can be viewed more as promotional or marketing initiatives that allow retailers to highlight sales in advertisements, specifically through circulars and coupons. This **gamification** prolongs the shopping experience, now starting at home with the customer planning purchases, cutting coupons, exploring websites or circulars, and building excitement for the upcoming trip to the mall or retailer. This planned discount is built into the profit margin, and even at 50 percent off, the retailer will still gain some amount of profit. Working down the supply chain, the profit margin is cut in half for the wholesale and for the manufacturer. To determine the discount selling price once the discount percentage is known, the formula is:

Original Retail Price − (Original Retail Price × Discount %) = New Discount Selling Price

Therefore if the original price is $90 and a 25 percent discount is to be applied, you will calculate it like this:

Original Retail Price − (Original Retail Price × Discount %) = New Discount Selling Price
$90 − ($90 × 25%) = New Discount Selling Price
$90 − ($90 × 0.25) = New Discount Selling Price
$90 − $22.50 = New Discount Selling Price
$90 − $22.50 = $67.50

And if the selling price is $49.95 and a $35 percent discount is to be applied, the discount formula will look like this:

Original Retail Price − (Original Retail Price × Discount %) = New Discount Selling Price
$49.95 − ($49.95 × 35%) = New Discount Selling Price
$49.95 − ($49.95 × 0.35) = New Discount Selling Price
$49.95 − $17.48 = New Discount Selling Price
$49.95 − $17.48 = $32.47

Markdowns

Markdowns are losses, but markdowns are also a strategy to bring customers to the store in order to clear out unsold merchandise. Discounts and markdowns are often advertised as big events.

Retailers who choose status or premium pricing strategies aim to sell products at full price and discourage sales of any sort for fear of tarnishing their brand. Markdowns of this sort are typically not visible to the customer within the first retail setting, the flagship store, or premium store. The product will be moved to the **outlet store**. It is important to note this is not always the case. Outlet stores have increased popularity, requiring brands to develop merchandise specifically for the outlet retail setting. Outlet stores are an important retail format for luxury brands to "discard" products that were not selling in the flagship stores. They mark down the prices, as opposed to having a sale at a certain percent. To determine the markdown percentage once the original retail price has been discounted to a markdown price, the formula is:

(Markdown Price − Original Retail Price) ÷ Original Retail Price = Markdown %

Therefore, if the original price is $90 and the store has marked the item down to $74, you can calculate the markdown percentage like this:

(Markdown Price − Original Retail Price) ÷ Original Retail Price = Markdown %
($74 − $90) ÷ $90 = Markdown %
(−$16) ÷ $90 = Markdown %
−$16 ÷ $90 = 0.1777
0.1777 = 17.77%
17.77% = Markdown %

And you can check your calculation by using the discount formula like this:

$$\text{Original Retail Price} - (\text{Original Retail Price} \times \text{Discount \%}) = \text{New Discount Selling Price}$$
$$\$90 - (\$90 \times 17.77\%) = \text{New Discount Selling Price}$$
$$\$90 - (\$90 \times 0.1777) = \text{New Discount Selling Price}$$
$$\$90 - \$15.99 = \text{New Discount Selling Price}$$
$$\$90 - \$15.99 = \$74.007$$

Chargebacks

Chargebacks, or reverse charges, occur when an error has taken place on the manufacturing, design, packaging, or delivery level. Throughout the design process, approval is required by the wholesaler and/or retailer. If standards are not met, both wholesalers and retailers have the ability to remit payment through chargebacks when invoicing. This can be severely damaging to the brand relationship and manufacturer relationship as well as to the profitability of the company.

An example of chargebacks may take place if a product is not packaged using the correct hanger and polybag when shipped to a large department store. Department stores are known for setting strict standards. Brands are encouraged to use DC's to avoid any unnecessary reverse charges. DC's can spot check measurements, coloring, quality, packaging and a whole host of other aspects in the effort to avoid chargebacks. Chargebacks are also incurred if orders are shipped late or incomplete. A chargeback amount can vary from 20 percent to 80 percent and is negotiable.

Markdowns, Discounts, and Chargebacks on the Cost Sheet

As not every item that enters a store or is listed on a website sells as soon as possible at the listed prices, all of these discounts, markdowns, and chargebacks are inevitable. Therefore, it is important to realize that for most brands, not all items will sell at full retail price, and they must be prepared for markdowns and loss. While companies attempt to manufacture the correct amount of styles, colors, patterns and sizes, it is generally a fact that for most, a certain percentage of sizes and colors remain unsold after the initial selling period or at the end of a season. They can defray this loss by adding a markdown percentage (also known as close-out percent) to their cost sheet, so that the reduction in price on a minority of styles is covered by the selling of the majority of styles. It is common practice for companies producing large quantities of many styles to add 1 percent to 2 percent to all styles to cover the future discounting that will occur. For smaller companies, they may wish to increase by 2–4 percent. This line item is titled Markdowns and Close-outs, and can be seen in the cost sheet (Table 7.1) that includes a line for the expectation of future unwanted merchandise.

Table 7.1 Anticipated markdowns are now loaded on to the traditional cost sheet

Traditional Cost Sheet					
Date		Company			
Style No.	Sxs No.	Season			Group
Size Range	Sxs Size	Description			
Fabric					
Fabric	**Est. Yield**	**@Est. $/yard**	**Est. Cost**	**Total Est. Cost**	**SKETCHES**
Fabric 1:					
Fabric 2:					
Freight:					
Trims	**Est. Quantity**	**@Est. $/ yard/gr/pc**	**Est. Cost**		
Trim 1:					
Trim 2:					
Trim 3:					
Freight:					**FRONT VIEW**
Notions	**Est. Quantity**	**@Est. $/ yard/gr/pc**	**Est. Cost**		
Notion 1:					
Notion 2:					
Freight:					
Labor	**Direct**	**Contract Work**			
Cutting:					
Sewing:					
Finishing:					
Marking/Grading:					
EST. First Cost of Goods					
Agent Commission %					
Est. Freight					
Duty %					
Clearance %					
Local Freight					**BACK VIEW**
Markdowns / Closeouts					
Total Misc Costs					
Est. LDP / DDP Cost					
Wholesale Markup		Markup Goal %	100%–MU%	Markup $	
Wholesale Price					
Retailer Markup		Markup Goal %	100%–MU%	Markup $	
Retailer Price					
Manufacturer's Suggested Retail Price (MSRP)					

Recording Profitability

Profitability can be analyzed by product or SKU, category, brand, season, and company. As previously mentioned, past financial information is the greatest tool to future economic success. It is important to analyze all aspects of the business to discover trends. Companies use **POS (Point of Sales) systems**, in order to pass along reports to the corporate office. Flagship stores serve as a centralized location to develop samples, test merchandise, and gather important financial data. With a quick click of a button, full reports analyzing everything from individual store performance, employee performance, to color performance can be sent to all company decision-makers across the globe for discussion and adjustment.

Meeting the Customer's Needs

The US customer has been conditioned to look for merchandise that is on sale. Out of the three main marketing tools: price, quality, and newness, price is the most important to the US market. Shopping on sale is about winning. As a consumer, I am winning and, in the eyes of the consumer, the retailer is losing when I receive 50 percent off on an item. In reality, we know at 50 percent off the retailer has built enough markup into the pricing to still retain at least a small amount of profit. Typically, retailers using the high-low pricing strategy will start to reduce prices seventeen–nineteen days after the merchandise hits the store. The customer must decide if the product is worth full price or if they are willing to risk returning in three weeks to find the item at a discount or sold out.

JC Penney is a prime example of a company that tried to eliminate sales from their strategy in favor of EDLP as well as move their target market from Baby Boomers to Millennials. JC Penney stores have a glut of inventory and falling stock prices in part due to the economic recession of 2007–2009. JC Penney tried to make a quick pivot by changing their name to JCP and offering a "square deal", which was further highlighted by their new square logo. The store was going to eliminate all sales, coupons, and other rewards in return for lower prices. Customers revolted. Customers have been conditioned to look for sales, cut coupons, and participate in what retailers call gamification. Taking away this interaction left the customer bored with the straightforward low prices. This and other initiatives failed quickly, and soon JCP returned to their traditional sales, coupons, and loyalty systems.

Winning the Profit Game

While there is no exact formula for finding and maintaining profitability, there are strategies and goals a company can set that will set them on the road to success. A product's life cycle begins with the introductory phase, followed by the growth phase, then maturity, and decline. During this cycle, one can hope they have stumbled upon a bestseller. Levi's 501 jeans are a classic staple in their collection that they can rely on season after season. Levi's is able to replenish this style quickly, avoiding PD costs associated with new styles. Levi's is also able to use data and trend reports to analyze their various products and categorize them by life cycle. For example, backpacks last season may have been in the introduction phase moving into the growth phase because Levi's added new colorways and styles. Perhaps as they near the decline phase, Levi's can pivot by expanding into a product extension offering a variety of different bags. As styles return each season, it is necessary to recost them each season as raw material and labor costs shift, along with freight, gasoline, and duty charges. A company is wise to recost and, if needed, reprice.

Another growth strategy is international expansion. Once again with increased technology and communication, retailers are able to access international markets. The largest companies in the world often have a retail footprint in a variety of countries that offer slightly different to very different products. This expansion is costly and must be done with precision, but it can lead to varying degrees of success.

Case Study: Using Existing Styles for Off-Price Divisions

As we have learned throughout the previous chapters, the off-price division is booming with sales and growing faster than ever. Many companies throughout the fashion industry create products specifically for this lower-priced category and particular market of customers. Many of these off-price consumers love the idea of buying a "designer" or a "brand name label", but at a very low price. Designers and fashion brands allow for these customers to buy into their name brand by offering only certain types of merchandise to off-price retailers like TJ Maxx or Ross Stores.

In order to achieve these low price points, designer and fashion houses will take existing styles from their previous collections and "re-issue" less expensive versions of these styles. These styles can be from past seasons, current best-sellers, or styles from their existing collection. However, in order to not confuse the main designer collection with the off-price merchandise, these companies will change different elements of their styles created only for the off-price distribution.

Certain aspects of this off-price style must be changed in order to hit the lower price point. The fabric, trims, construction details, cost of labor, and overall quality will be changed in order to reduce costs. By making these slight variations, the total cost will be reduced, allowing for this company to sell the merchandise at a much lower price to this off-price target customer.

For example, a major fashion company sells a very popular men's woven button-down shirt. This company has a very strong brand heritage and sells their cotton poplin button-down men's shirts at full-price retailers anywhere from $89.50 to $98.50. They offer the button-down shirt in slim as well as classic fits. The material of this shirt is 100 percent cotton or may have a bit of spandex for added stretch (making it 98 percent cotton/2 percent spandex) and is constructed with expensive stitching details and seam finishes. The construction utilizes single-needle topstitching, and the lines of stitching are closely laid next to each other to form a strong seam to secure the fabric of the garment pattern pieces. This means there is only one row of stitching to avoid puckering or a bubbling effect at the seams and also the buttonholes are hand-stitched to avoid fraying over time. There is an iconic logo embroidered in the middle of the left chest pocket to show off the brand insignia. This embroidered logo utilizes multiple color threads to give dimension and texture to the brand's logo design. In addition, if the shirt has a pattern like a check or stripe, the patterns match at the seams and where the pocket is attached to the front, and there is not an obvious shift of this pattern configuration. There may also be a yoke at the back body for added support or back darts to give a better shape of the garment against the body. Also, the actual buttons on this shirt placket and sleeves utilize shell or mother-of-pearl quality buttons with an engraving of the brand name. The shirt may be assembled, sewn, and shipped from a country of higher labor costs, such as America or Italy.

However, this same designer brand can basically knock itself off and make the same exact shirt using different materials and by removing and revising the expensive construction details. They would sell this particular style from the main collection, but at a much lower price point of $29.99. By using a less expensive quality fabric that may be blended with a synthetic fiber, such as polyester, the price of the fabric per yard has already dropped down. In addition, using a cheaper quality button like plastic and use a faux-shell design, as opposed to actual shell also further drives down the costs. Removing the engraving of the brand name also makes the button cost less expensive. In addition to using less expensive fabrics and trims, the off-price version of this shirt would become less expensive when the construction details are further compromised. The quality would still be up to the designer's standard but it could be produced at a manufacturing facility that has less expensive labor rates, such as India, China, or Vietnam. The removal of construction details like the back darts, back yoke, collar stands, collar stays and less expensive stitching details not only would make the shirt less expensive but the fit would also be differentiated from the top-tier shirt that sells at a much higher price point. In addition, we could also remove the chest pocket, but keep the iconic brand logo. The brand logo embroidered at the chest would only use one color thread, as opposed to multiple colors in the original top-tier designer style. Finally, the brand would ensure that the body colorways offered in this style would not be the same current colors being used or shown on the runway.

By changing all these different elements of the original style, designers basically can get away with producing similar garments at a much lower price point. This allows for designers and fashion labels to offer a range of products to many different types of consumers and tap into the off-price market to gain sales from a target market they normally would not be servicing.

Case Study: Amazon Case Study

Introduction

Technological innovations have created many disruptions in the retail industry resulting in bankruptcies and closures. No other company has benefited the most than Amazon. Known for their large product offerings and speedy delivery, it is not surprising that they have become the first trillion-dollar company. Looking back at their success, Amazon began by selling books, later moving to electronics, and now almost anything can be found on Amazon. They began this behemoth of a company by "beating out" the competition. Category killers enter the market, undercutting their competition by buying a single product category in bulk thus being able to offer lower prices. Amazon was able to succeed against new and used book retailers not only by providing lower prices but also with the use of data collection and price sensitive algorithms.

Data Collection

Buying a product online is much more than a convenient way to shop. Buying online is now a means for retailers, marketers, and perhaps nefarious characters to collect information. This information is used to create customer profiles allowing the brand access and information to our personal preferences and habits. Target, with their extensive customer profiles, has even been able to predict pregnancies long before the customer is thinking about purchasing a bottle or diaper. It is obvious companies will use this information to send coupons to incentivize customers, but Amazon has taken the use of data collection to the next level. Amazon can analyze the times customers do the bulk of their shopping, what day of the week they prefer to purchase certain items, and therefore make assumptions on how to best use this information to their advantage. This information is then used to adjust pricing using custom algorithms.

Price-Sensitive Algorithm

Amazon can change a price of an item as many times throughout the day as they would like. Instead of taking the traditional high-low approach to pricing, Amazon works from the bottom-up. Amazon can select a price with a very small margin with the goal of selling a large volume of product. As discussed in the chapter, most companies will sell with a markup of 40–70 percent, but Amazon will select a low markup, as little as 20 percent or lower, undercutting the market and gaining more market share. Through data collection and custom algorithms, Amazon may discover a customer or group of customers browsing women's coats consistently on Wednesday afternoons. This information can give Amazon the tools to either offer greater discounts, increase the price, or offer coupons depending on further analytics. It is ironic that Amazon, which first began online wiping out the physical retail-store competition in the 2000's, is now beginning to open its own brick and mortar stores.

Brick and Mortar

Ask any customer what percentage of shopping the average American does online and most will come anywhere close to 9 percent. Most Americans still want to visit a physical store to select their fruit and vegetables as well as "purchase" the whole experience of buying a luxury bag. With this information, it is not surprising that Amazon is opening brick and mortar stores. Amazon's physical locations that offer best-selling books and the fleet of their smart electronics have got customers scratching their heads as to why the largest retailer would take the added fixed costs to open a store. Amazon knows that in order to continue to gain more market share from their competitors, omni-channel distribution is important to convert the internet-illiterate customer. Amazon also gathers important insight into this customer.

Conclusion

Amazon continues to strengthen its business by continuous purchasing competitors and by adding product offerings and services to grow its portfolio. Amazon's acquisition of Whole Foods in 2017 was a testament to their success because of the one-day stock price increase that covered the cost of the acquisition. Amazon continues to strive for continued success by pouring funds into their Alexa services. Alexa, a smart assistant, answers many questions and commands from turning on the light to creating grocery lists, or going a step further and creating a basket with the mostly private-label Amazon product offerings. Even with customer complaints of Alexa recording conversations unprompted, there seems to be no backlash from customers.

Discussion Questions

- You have a newly launched website to sell books and other reading materials. You traditionally have sold through brick and mortar locations. Your customers enjoy your low prices and you have a national brand presence and great reputation. Your markup is rather fair at a 50 percent markup from the wholesale price. If you bought the book at a wholesale price of $12.50 from a particular publisher, what would be your retail price? In addition, what would be the final amount of retail dollars that was generated after you sold this book to exactly 100,000 customers online.

- From here, imagine you are Amazon and you purchase the same exact book at a wholesale price of $12.50. However, you sell your books at a very low price point with only a 25 percent wholesale markup. In addition, you have a huge reach to millions of online customers. Thus far, you have sold this book to 650,000 customers worldwide. What is the amount of retail dollars generated from Amazon sales of this book? Do you see the correlation to the above case study and difference in pricing structures?

Summary

Achieving profitability and finding the right profit margin is as essential as finding the right fit of the garment or the right customer for your product. Margins are the differences between selling price/revenue and profit. Margins are what is left for the company to grow.

Markups are the differences between costs/expenses and selling price/revenue. Markups are what is added to cost. Both are important, and you can select target markup based on what you want your margin to be.

Markdowns, discounts, and chargebacks eat away at profit and lower the margin from the target markup. It is wise to include a markdown percent on a cost sheet to cover all discounts, markdowns, returns, and chargebacks that may apply after goods are shipped.

It is very important to pay attention to the needs of your market and customers. The US customer has been conditioned to look for merchandise that is on sale; therefore, many businesses profit from the high-low approach.

A company's awareness of the life cycle phases of their various products is crucial to their profitability. Adjusting your line as your products go through the cycle of introduction, growth, maturity, and decline will help offset losses incurred, as certain products inevitably remain on the shelf.

Chapter Review and Discussion

1. Imagine you have a clothing brand with a collection of ten–twelve styles. Your average profit markup across the line is 55 percent. Two styles only have a 30 percent and 35 percent markup added to the total costs. What are five reasons that styles may receive such a low markup and still bring the company good profitability?
2. Why might a company add a 78 percent markup to a style and in the end have only earned a 23 percent margin.
3. What are the reasons that a retailer might request chargeback dollars for partial or full garment orders?
4. What are reasons that products are discounted and marked down? How can a manufacturer prepare for this possibility?
5. Why might a retail store like the Gap have difficulty with its customer base if they announced plans to shift toward an EDLP model?

Activities and Exercises

1. Search this item online: a grey Champion-brand hooded sweatshirt. Look up and list all the e-tailers that the hoodie is selling at right now, with their selling prices. How many different prices did you find the hoodie selling at? Why do you think there are such a diverse variety of prices and stores selling this item? If you read the fiber, fabric, detail descriptions of each hoodie at each different price, what are the differences (if any) from price to price and why?

2. Turn to a classmate and imagine they are the manager of a button factory in Canada. You want to order 100 gross of their 36L cedar-wood sew-through buttons for a coat you are producing. The buttons cost $22.00/gross. You need to bring your costs down. How do you ask your Canadian button supplier classmate to lower their price, so you can make a great profit margin on this style? Practice negotiating with them and attempt to get the buttons for 10 percent less. What is your plea? What tone of voice do you use? Then reverse the roles. What cost-negotiation questions, statements, techniques worked best and why?

3. If you have a style with a retail selling price of $259.99 and have a 25 percent off sale, what will the discount selling price be? What will the price be if instead you apply a 36 percent discount?

Key Terms

direct-to-consumer
gamification
markdown

omni-channel
outlet store
POS system (point of sales)

8 Ways to Cut Costs

There are a number of ways to cut costs throughout the PD, manufacturing, and overall supply chain process. Cutting costs is sometimes required in order to meet the target price the consumer will accept, to achieve a competitive advantage against the competition, and to minimize initial investment if you are a new designer. Examining cost-cutting techniques is of interest to all fashion and related businesses even when none of these pertain to the situation; because of the often-unpredictable nature of the fashion industry, a company never knows what factors could help or hinder sales. Due to globalization and the interconnectedness of companies, supply chains, and markets around the world, price changes can occur quickly and without warning. Having a plan in place to work with these changes can result in the success or failure of a company. Let's begin at the development stage to examine where and how costs can be cut.

It Starts with the Sample

All styles are not created the same. Some styles are dreamed up by a designer after visiting a fashion show or museum, and many styles are generated from the research conducted using costly trend analysis databases. Other styles are simply copied. The former example requires a designer or product developer to draw a sketch and find a sample maker, ideally the designer will have a sample maker on hand. Together they will work to perfect the fit, construction, and silhouette. This used to be the reality for most designers, but with our always-connected world and the need to drive down prices, designers often copy or adapt already-existing garments. Shopping trips are a common occurrence in research, where designers visit nearby department stores, purchase garments that are close to the design they hope to achieve, and send them to overseas factories to basically knock off the design. Not as glamorous as the first example, this process gets the job done faster and with a significant discount. It is important to note that this process may cut back costs during this phase of development, but it requires a larger investment later on because of minimum orders required by the manufacturer, which we will examine in greater detail later on in this chapter.

Watering Down the Line

Moving through the development process, as we examined in Chapter 2, the fit process is composed of a series of comments and garments between the patternmaker, technical designer, and product developer in order to achieve the desired design. The initial sketch or CAD may have elaborate seams, appliques, pleating, and more. As the garment is being fit, the production team is simultaneously working with the factory to cost the garment. It is not an uncommon occurrence for the production team to ask the design team to remove expensive trims or "water down" the collection overall to meet the target price. Many agents or factory managers may also suggest reducing the number seams or stitches per inch. Fewer small stitches means faster sewing and fewer **SAMs (standard applied minutes)**. Fewer SAMs equals less cost. Thus, 3.5 SAMs for a shirt translates to three and one-half minutes to complete the sewing of one shirt. Each serged side seam, attached neck band, and double-needle hem stitched is 0.5 SAMs (or thirty seconds each). A factory measures and calculates SAMs to determine the CMT cost (Kennedy, 2017). Reducing SAMs is one way to bring down cost. Other examples of simplifying the processes to reduce costs include the following:

- Changing from a French seam or flat-felled seam to an edge-stitched or serged seam finish.
- Changing from triple- or double-needle topstitching to a single-needle topstitch or edgestitch.
- Omitting hand-stitched and hand-finished features and switching them to machine-sewn details, which are faster to complete.
- Removing flaps, pleats, or closures from pockets.
- Engineering markers to use selvedges as the seam edges, and therefore eliminating seam finishes along those edges.
- Switching from being a fully-lined garment to a partially-lined garment.
- Reducing the amounts of buttons and buttonholes, or snaps, hook-n-eyes, etc.
- Reducing the amounts of tucks, pleats, darts, or gathers.
- Reducing the total number of colors, prints, or patterns in which a style is produced.
- Switching from numerical sizing (i.e., 6, 8, 20, 12, and 14) to S/M/L sizing and reducing the number of total sizes sent to production.

Search online for "Fashion Studies Journal, Right-Brained Fashion" for the full article on approaching costs savings creatively, or follow the QR code here.

The Cost Is in the Fabric

The fabric typically can be the largest cost associated with the garment. It is common for the fabric to be one-sixth to one-eighth of the total price of the garment retail price. When the cost of a garment is too high the fabric is usually the first place to look. The type of fabric, fiber content, dying process, and weight are all on the chopping block. Ways to reduce fabric costs include:

- Changing from 100 percent of a particular fiber to a blend.
- Changing a natural fiber to a lower-priced synthetic option, while a good cost-cutting practice, this makes a garment less sustainable, as new synthetic fabrics are derived from fossil fuels, more on this topic in Chapter 9.
- Switching from a yarn-dyed stripe, check, or other pattern to a printed stripe, check, etc.
- Selecting a slightly lighter-weight fabric.
- Choosing a fabric with a lesser thread count.
- Reducing the number of colors in a print. The more colors, the more screens or cylinders.
- Sourcing deadstock (unused, often old, and generally marked down) fabric instead of producing new cloth.

- Selecting a fabric that originates from a country or region closer to the factory, thereby reducing freight costs.
- Switching from a one-way or engineered print or pattern to a two-way print or all-over print, which consume less yardage per style.
- Reducing the yield of fabric per style by making the style slightly less roomy, or removing fabric-intensive details, such as gather, pleats, deep pockets, etc.

With the exception of using deadstock fabric, with many of these cost-cutting ways, quality generally suffers; and garment longevity is not achieved and with so many companies cutting costs with lighter-weight fabrics, it is no wonder that many fast fashion companies sell garments that are literally see-through when held to the light.

Those Trims and Notions Add up Too

Trimmings, notions, and findings add up. Often, companies will look at reducing their labor and fabric costs without realizing the savings in the reducing or changing of trims, hangtags, labels, and similar items. Options on reducing trim and notions costs include:

- Reducing the amounts of closures (buttons, snaps, and hook-n-eyes).
- Eliminating the extra button on a coat, jacket or shirt, or the extra yarn on a sweater.
- Reusing existing or vintage buttons or trims, as opposed to purchasing new.
- Selecting a slightly narrower trim, for example, a narrower draw cord or braid.
- Switching to a lighter-weight trim, for example, a plastic instead of metal zipper.
- Using fusible interfacing inside of lapels, collars, and pocket flaps instead traditional stitches.
- Reducing the number of colors in a screen, heat-applied vinyl, or glitter print trim.
- Reducing the number of rhinestone/bead colors or embroidery thread colors in a design.
- Shift from individually stitched hook-n-eyes or snaps, to hook-n-eye or snap tape that is machine sewn.
- Printing the label inside of a garment instead of purchasing and stitching labels.

One good way to lower cost is to simplify the overall design to a less labor-intensive style, and to reduce the number of total components, as every component adds costs and time in sourcing, ordering, tracking, and receiving. Of course, we all do not want to stroll around in one-color basic shifts. The beauty of fashion is the beauty of the design and the creative ways to utilize fabric, sewing skills, and trims. But if your goal is to cost less, the best way to get there is use all of those wonderful factors less as well.

Negotiations with Vendors

Another cost-cutting technique is negotiating with the vendor. The manufacturer or sourcing agent used may be just as important as the design selection. The relationships built throughout the supply chain are instrumental to the success of the brand and should not be taken for granted. The vendor you work with and negotiate with wants to problem-solve with you, but they must also ensure they are able to profit and stay in business themselves. Your supply chain partners (you should think of them as partners) also have a large team that must be paid and who also depend on the success of their company. With that said, vendors might be open to giving a better price for one style with the promise of increasing the order or not negotiating for the lowest price on another style. It is worth mentioning again that it is all about relationships. It is the production manager's job to get the lowest price and the vendor's job to push for a fairer price without damaging the relationship. It is important to give and take when it comes to delivery dates, labor costs, and especially if a fabric, trim, or design mistake is made that is irreversible. It is not uncommon to have to receive goods that are imperfect in order to maintain the relationship, but it is certainly common to ask for a reduction in price for those materials.

Negotiating is constant in the wholesale apparel market. A brand negotiates with their fabric mills and sewing and knitting factories, and with a trade show management company for a booth to display their lines, by asking for a lower booth price per square foot. In turn, retailers negotiate with fashion brands for special rates and for advertising that they sell a particular brand. It is often difficult to meet a desired target margin and make on average that sweet keystone margin of 50 percent, even after we have paid all our bills, taxes, expenses, and commissions.

Negotiating and Reducing Costs to Achieve Profit Margin

Back in Chapter 1, we discussed a Victorian-themed blouse. If the landed cost of the blouse is $20.71, and we knew we needed to sell that blouse at approximately $38.00 retail, that would only give allow us to make a 45.5 percent markup, assuming no items are discounted

---

Retail – Cost / Retail = MarkUp
$38.00 − $20.71 = $17.29
$17.29 ÷ $38.00 = 0.455
0.455 = 45.5%

A profit of 45.5 percent for a fashion style is not desirable, and we revised the style details, fit, materials, and workmanship to lower the costs. There is another method to lowering cost and that is to negotiate. Negotiation occurs with suppliers of raw materials, cutting, sewing, knitting, and finishing factories, sourcing and factory agents, packaging suppliers, and shippers. Pretty much every cost can be negotiated except for US duties, customs, and port of entry fees.

Companies *do* want your business, and will generally be somewhat willing to negotiate in order to secure that business. Of course, new companies negotiating with first-time suppliers, services, and factories will most likely just be able to negotiate a small percent. The longer your relationship with a company, the better prices you will be quoted. Negotiating takes skill, and often the answer will be that you are already receiving the best price. But as intimidating as it may be to ask again, it is always suggested to ask your suppliers to sharpen their prices and help you achieve your cost. The only place it is not recommended to negotiate is the garment workers' pay. For reasons of business ethics, we should all work toward fair pay for all workers, wherever they are located along the supply chain. In studies by Oxfam it was revealed that, on average, between 2 percent and 4 percent of the price of a piece of clothing sold covers a garment factory workers' wages. Similarly, there is research by the Asia Floor Wage Alliance that "between 0.5% and 3% of the cost of a garment at retail goes to the worker who made it" (Asia Floor Wage Alliance, 2017).

And in Bangladesh, Vietnam, and Indonesia, the average wages are a quarter to half of what is considered a living wage (Nayeem and Kyriacou, 2017). With fashion factory workers being paid so little all around the globe, it is truly unethical to negotiate further on sewing labor rates. Search online for "Asia Floor Wage" and "Oxfam, What She Makes", or follow the QR codes here for further details on ethical wages.

It is better to negotiate on materials and similar line items that are the greater costs of your styles. It is best to first research the costs from other suppliers so you are well informed before you begin to ask for a lower price, and it is always suggested to present your plea as one that can be mutually beneficial; that is, for a fiber supplier, like Repreve, you may offer to market for the business by putting their logo on your hang tag or on your website in return for a 10 percent reduction in fabric costs. Generally, the larger the order, the better your chance of fruitful negotiations.

Successful negotiating at several different line items can bring your total landed costs down by at least 4–14 percent. With negotiations, a company may very well reduce the Victorian-themed blouse by an average of 9 percent. That would bring the landed cost to $18.85. With a target selling price of $38.00, the profit is now increased to 50.4 percent, which is a keystone markup and allows for a much more sustainable profit.

Retail − Cost / Retail = MarkUp
$38.00 − $18.85 = $19.15
$19.15 ÷ $38.00 = 0.504
0.504 = 50.4%

With sharper negotiations, the profit could increase by around 1–3 percent more.

And What about Indirect Cost-Cutting?

Changing the fabric, buttons, or number of pin tucks are all ways to reduce the materials and construction costs of direct cost line items. But what about all those indirect costs, as discussed in earlier chapters? The ideal way to make a greater margin is to evaluate those lunch meeting costs, uber rides to appointments, and wild amounts of sample fabric, trim, and garment orders that all designers love to make. By reducing overhead and overhead percent, you can increase profit without style quality, design beauty, and diversity suffering. This is important because cost-cutting to just meet a price allows for a potentially poorly-made garment to arrive at a store of such quality that it is returned. Returned items require chargebacks, and chargebacks equal loss. All the more reason to look at your indirect costs and expenses under a magnifying glass and omit the extraneous. To help insure your products are not returned, always build in tests for seam strength (can you can pull the garment apart at the seams?), launderability (measure it, wash it, dry it, and measure it again!), and colorfastness (wash it, dry it, and check the color matching on all components). Quality test and inspections from start to finish will allow a company to avoid paying for rework and reject fees and those dreaded chargebacks.

Case Study: A. Bernadette

A. Bernadette, a start-up sustainable fashion brand, uses a variety of cost-cutting methods to cut back on expenses, but also to reduce its environmental imprint. Creating a line from scratch can produce a lot of waste when deciding what fabric to use, creating samples, and from the dreaded unsold product. It is important to A. Bernadette's brand identity to reduce, reuse, and recycle as well as remain transparent to its customers and stakeholders. Let's take a closer look at these cost savings techniques.

Line Development

Slow fashion, a new type of line development in response to fast fashion, requires the designer to take careful consideration, thus slowing down the process when deciding who, what, where, when, and how the product will be made. Capsule collections, curated lines consisting of basic items— skirt, shirt, pant, shorts, to name a few—have grown in popularity. Geared toward the minimalist, conscious consumer, this collection also benefits the designer. Season after season, the designer can keep the same silhouettes and change the fabric or make modifications to the existing line, thus cutting back on the waste associated with PD.

Pattern-Making

Producing new silhouettes can be costly and challenging if the right team is not in place. Designers must understand fabric characteristics, and pattern makers are instrumental to the fit and construction of the garment. Without these key players and the budget to hire professionals, a line can take much longer than anticipated to create. It is advised to create slopers, basic patterns, which can be manipulated to develop other styles. Spending time with a pattern maker to create slopers, and samples from the slopers will save time and money down the road. Many designers skip this step because of their eagerness to see their designs come to life. Similar to painting a room, producing a collection is 90 percent preparation and 10 percent actual sewing and production. Taking a pattern-making class is advisable to learn how to correct your own patterns. A. Bernadette began their recent collection by first hosting a line planning party. Friends and family were measured and analyzed to develop the styles and sizes. New designers first customers are often those within their network. Next, A. Bernadette produced samples and invited friends and family again to fit the garments. Although these people were not professional fit models, A. Bernadette knew the value added when including customers in the experience of creating a line.

Upcycled Fabric

More and more upcycled fabric is becoming available for designers to use. After collections are made, large design companies throw away 15 percent of their fabric. This fabric can end up in a landfill even if brand new. One company, FABSCRAP, is trying to remove textile waste from the waste stream in New York City. FABSCRAP provides a service to large and small designers to pick up no-longer-needed fabric and transport it to their warehouse in Brooklyn for sorting. Pure 100 percent fiber fabric, for example 100 percent wool or 100 percent cotton, is easier to recycle, while blended fabric is harder. Students, sustainable advocates, and crafters visit FABSCRAP to help sort fabric in return for 5 pounds (2.2 kilograms) of fabric for free. A. Bernadette volunteered over the course of a summer and was able to bring 50 pounds (22.5 kilograms) of fabric to Uganda for sampling. Creating designs from upcycled fabric can come with a number of challenges, but designers are meeting the challenge by engineering their patterns to eliminate any waste, also known as **zero waste pattern-making.** Search online for "FABSCRAP", or follow the QR code here to found out more.

Designing for the Customer

Taking all three of these techniques, line development, pattern-making, and upcycled fabric into account, the overall theme is customer-centricity. Slowing down the process allows a designer to constantly gather information from the customer, resulting in a better product and fewer unsold items. It is more important than ever to include your customer in the design process, answer the question, "Who made your clothing?," and do so in an authentic, transparent manner.

Summary

Some styles are dreamed up by a designer after visiting a fashion show or museum and many styles are generated from the research conducted using costly trend analysis databases – and all begin with a sample. From sample to production, the material, trims, and even design can be altered to cut costs.

Another cost-cutting technique is negotiating with the vendor. Negotiating is constant in the apparel market, and the longer you are in business, the better your negotiating power and the friendlier your relationships. Textile factory employees and other below-the-line workers are your partners as well, and they must be properly compensated for financial and ethical sustainability.

The ideal way to make a greater margin is to evaluate those lunch meeting costs, uber rides to appointments, and wild amounts of sample fabric, trim, and garment orders that all designers love to place. The day-to-day necessities of business don't come free.

Finally, knowing that your products are always made and shipped to your specifications ensures that chargebacks will be few and far between. The best offense is a good defense, and if you know that your garments are always stitched perfectly and always go through the washer and dryer without shrinking or losing their vibrance, your costs will cut themselves.

Chapter Review and Discussion

1. Which three people are most involved in the "fit" process, what are their roles, and are these people each direct or indirect cost factors?
2. What is the relationship between tracking SAMs and the CMT cost?
3. Why might a company switch from numerical sizes to S/M/L to reduce cost?
4. How could the old phrase *less is more* be applied to cost-cutting and sustainability practices?
5. What is the limit to cutting costs? Should the bottom line be valued over professional relationships or ethical concerns?
6. Why does a larger order size sometimes reduce the need to cut costs?

Activities and Exercises

1. As a designer or a product developer, you have a particular jacket style that must arrive at a target cost of $45 total for fabric, trims, and notions used in this garment's production. This outerwear style is utilizing a shell fabric made of 100 percent lambswool suiting fabric from Italy, a lining made of 100 percent silk, a name-brand metal zipper, and button closures for inside pockets. In addition, there are sleeve headers, shoulder pads and fusible at the pocket openings and lapels. Moreover, there are four separate labels that are being used for branding, the COO, sizing, and care labels. Currently, you are landing at $60, which is $15 over the budget. What are some different methods that you learned in this chapter to manage lowering your target cost price? How can you bring down your costs through different methods of cutting costs? Create an outline of possible solutions or methods to apply to reducing your target cost.

2. Take a look at a suit jacket, blazer, parka, or motorcycle jacket. Notice the interfacing in the collars, the lining, and all the details. If you were the designer of this jacket, what changes could you make to reduce the price by $20.00 at retail? Ponder those changes. Would the piece still have the same quality? Look? Fit? Do all these direct cost factors add value to the style?

3. Consider the SAM value of these three shirt styles: a basic tee = three–five SAMs; a standard polo = six–twelve SAMs; a tuxedo shirt = twenty–thirty SAMs. What makes each style have these specific SAMs? Think about the price of each. Does the average pricing coincide with the average SAMs? Why?

Key Terms

deadstock   zero-waste patternmaking

9 Costing for Today's Sustainably Minded Market

Everywhere we look, large and small brands are highlighting sustainable initiatives and/or incorporating CSR (Corporate Social Responsibility) programs into their strategies. Sustainability is an urgent movement, and there are many ways a brand can include more sustainable business practices into their design, development, production, and distribution. Most sustainable practices are viewed at first as cost-increasing, but it is important to realize that they can and generally do save money and create profit in the long term.

In the very first paragraph of the introduction we wrote, "In this ever-changing fashion world, even the most seasoned fashion professionals cannot continue to cost the same way as they always have." It is imperative that everyone in the industry, or entering into the fashion trade, realize that nothing we do in fashion, including the ways we cost, can remain the same. Companies can no longer cost garments and products where the focus is on ever-increasing profit, without regard to the impact on communities, people, and waterways around the planet. The old model has led to a world that is business first and biodiversity last.

Fashion is a creative industry, it is a field where designers and merchandisers play with color, texture, line, patterns, prints, and shape. New fabric technology has given designers a burst of excitement and energy. Leftover orange peels are being turned into thread, kombucha-based bacteria is being grown to create fabric, and offcuts—leftover fabric from sampling or production—are being made available to young and upcoming designers. There is hope, and a revitalized sense of creativity is present in an industry that often feels repetitive and homogenized.

Pertaining to costing, perhaps it is time we stop hunching over cost sheets and crunching numbers, and instead look up and look out at ways in which we can also measure profit aside from the bottom lines of our income statements, as we advise you to do in Chapter 1. Increase in expenses is not always a negative. Customers are looking for products and brands that match their values and create opportunities around the world. Fair trade, the practice of adding a premium (additional costs to meet the living wage standards) to the labor costs, creates opportunities such as building schools, health care, and other social initiatives that help develop communities and local economies. This is one practice where people, brands, and customers win.

We suggest throughout this book to keep adding line items to your cost sheets. You cover your costs for Direct Factory Sourcing and PD, as well as for Markdowns and Close-outs. We suggest this approach so that your business can go forward and sustain itself and all its employees for the long term. When all costs are considered, you are not leaving money on the table, and whatever profit margin you earn has covered many of what is needed to cover. What remains is enough to propel a company forward.

Well the same is with today's focus on sustainability. A line item must be added that covers not only our doing-business-as-usual costs but also costs to produce positively upon this earth. We must still track costs and measure gain by ensuring expenses and costs are covered, but we must also add a line item for working toward the well-being of all people across our planet, and toward creating and implementing programs and management for clean water, air, land, and habitats across the globe.

Fashion is a large and complex global industry with thousands of different worldwide supply chain networks that produce and fly, float, and deliver components and products of every type to every corner of the world.

The quest for cutting costs and ever-increasing profits has led to externalizing the costs. Externalizing the cost means that other people in unseen places have had to pay these costs that the business did not. Students often enter the workforce to discover that their values and ethics are different than those of the corporation.

The ways businesses design, produce, and distribute products have aided in the decline of life quality for many places across the world, and greatly contributed to human-caused climate change. Just as indirect costs are listed and tracked, so must indirect impacts. There are other ways to measure profits. And in a book about cost sheets, where top and bottom lines, markup formulas, overhead percentages, margins, SAMs, activity pools, duty rates, and direct costs are discussed, we must also address these quality-of-life and responsibility-to-the-planet matters when costing garments. Many fashion and related businesses are now sustainably-minded, and so too are the customers. A few of the fashion companies that are profitable and driving this change are Patagonia, Levi's, Pact Apparel, Everlane, Eileen Fisher, Mara Hoffman, and Reformation.

These companies, and the many others doing their share, know that creating a responsible and sustainable product costs more. They have to raise their prices a bit in order to do the good things they do—especially at first. Often, the higher initial costs lead to a later reduction. The same is true with using repurposed waste that was destined for landfill (e.g., shipping orders with recycled boxes). Once sustainable practices and processes are infused and in place, true sustainability no longer costs more. And when it does, on average, the increased costs are balanced by the benefit of largely increased visibility, positive buzz, and increased sales.

Cutting costs, as we suggest in Chapter 8, is how the industry has evolved to create inexpensive, lesser quality, and poorly-fitting merchandise with fast workmanship. The industry has polluted the air and water along the way; extracted petroleum for new plastic buttons or polyester fabrics; and worked farmers, finishers, and sewers extremely hard without breaks and without providing respectable living wages. We must start to add these externalized costs on to our cost sheets. These are not tangible items for purchase that we can assign a dollar value.

So if we are not paying for them, how can we track them? Can we assign a value on a cost sheet for these externalized costs? Yes, we can internalize these costs so our cost sheets cover them, in the same manner as we can load PD costs on to cost sheets. As we slowly implement sustainable fibers, programs, or practices, we can track those costs. When work to reverse negative social and environmental impacts are input on a cost sheet, garments will cost a bit more, but those styles will be created with less carbon dioxide and toxic chemicals and will be zero waste and fair trade. When they are true, they can be marketed and will drive sales.

What we must do is work on adding responsible practices, and track those as we do our direct, indirect, fixed, and variable costs.

The expenses can be tracked by season/quarter/year and then tallied. They of course can be paid from the markup. But as repeatedly mentioned, that markup has to pay so much that little is left afterwards as profit—often just 10–15 percent.

Therefore, in today's world, where all companies should share in the responsibility to pollute less, practice water stewardship, use renewable energy, and utilize less natural resources for the growing population, an allowance should be added to the cost sheet to cover the added costs for any programs or initiatives put into place.

It is advisable, in order to be future-thinking, that the cost sheet be loaded with a line item for any/all sustainable/ethical practices that are in place. The practice of adding sustainability to a cost sheet is what we refer to as **eco-loading**. Eco-loading ensures that the purchase of an item helps pay for programs that will improve the lives of those who made the item, and fund environmental programs and offset programs to counteract any harm that was done in the creation of the item. To eco-load, the total anticipated amount of fees, wages, and expenses for the season or year for any/all programs rolled out along a company's supply chain, office, or selling spaces should be tallied, then divided by the anticipated revenue of the company for the same period, based on the previous season/year. Assuming a mid-sized

Chart 9.1 Example of how a company charts, lists, calculates, and keeps track of total sustainability and implementation costs of all types across all properties.

Sustainability Costs Tracking Sheet		
Initiative Description	Locale	Total Costs
Greenhouse Gas reduction / Renewable energy Program: _____ Goal/Targets: _____ _____	Office/Showroom/Studio	
	Warehouse/DC/brand-owned stores	
	Brand-owned transport	
	Mills/factories	
Energy reduction Program: _____ Goal/targets: _____ _____	Office/showroom/studio	
	Warehouse/DC/brand-owned stores	
	Brand-owned transport	
	Mills/factories	
Water conservation Program: _____ Goal/targets: _____ _____	Office/showroom/studio	
	Warehouse/DC/brand-owned stores	
	Brand-owned transport	
	Mills/factories	
Waste reduction / Recycling Program: _____ Goal/targets: _____ _____	Office/showroom/studio	
	Warehouse/DC/brand-owned stores	
	Brand-owned transport	
	Mills/factories	
Healthy materials / Detoxification Program: _____ Goal/targets: _____ _____	Office/showroom/studio	
	Warehouse/DC/brand-owned stores	
	Brand-owned transport	
	Mills/factories	
Agriculture / Forestry Program: _____ Goal/targets: _____ _____	Office/showroom/studio	
	Warehouse/DC/brand-owned stores	
	Brand-owned transport	
	Mills/factories	

Virgin plastic / petrol-chem reduction Program: _____ Goal/targets: _____ _____	Office/showroom/studio	
	Warehouse/DC/brand-owned stores	
	Brand-owned transport	
	Mills/factories	
Eco-Certifications / Compliance / Organizations Program: _____ Goal/targets: _____ _____	Office/showroom/studio	
	Warehouse/DC/brand-owned stores	
	Brand-owned transport	
	Mills/factories	
Fair Living Wage Program: _____ Goal/targets: _____ _____	Office/showroom/studio	
	Warehouse/DC/brand-owned stores	
	Brand-owned transport	
	Mills/factories	
SDG alignment Program: _____ Goal/targets: _____ _____	Office/showroom/studio	
	Warehouse/DC/brand-owned stores	
	Brand-owned transport	
	Mills/factories	
Offsetting Program: _____ Goal/targets: _____ _____	Office/showroom/studio	
	Warehouse/DC/brand-owned stores	
	Brand-owned transport	
	Mills/factories	
Grand Total Sustainability Costs		

company had a sales revenue of $900,000 in 2018 and plans to spend $40,000 in 2019 on certifications, training and a waterless dyeing initiative, the calculation of will look like this

Sustainable/Ethical Program Total $ ÷ Sales = Eco-Loading % $40,000 ÷ $900,000 = 0.444 0.444 = 4.4%

In this case, if 4.4 percent is added to the cost of all items, whether the item is a pair of $25 earmuffs, $75 khakis, or a $300 coat, a fraction is going toward environmental and social equity. This is a marketing opportunity that can be advertised on hangtags, labels, and social media pages. Just as those eating out in California have a 3–4 percent fee added to checks to cover healthcare for the restaurant's workers, so do garments of this new age.

A cost sheet that is loaded with sourcing, PD, and markdown allowances, along with a line for sustainable practices, is truly reflective of the price of fashion for today's changing world: a world in which a company must be profitable in order to do good things for the world and all their stakeholders.

Here is the new cost sheet Table 9.1, which includes the eco-loading factor.

Programs that can be put often spring from the Triple Bottom Line (TBL). The TBL places equal importance on three factors: economic, environmental, and social aspects of the company. A company can use the TBL as a strategy and set goals for each of the three sectors to work toward a goal and measure profit in each area in a variety of ways, including the following:

1. **Environmental**. Here profit is measured by environmental equity and justice programs that are implemented and that show progress in terms of how much they reduce the use and pollution of natural resources, and work toward clean air, water stewardship, and biodiversity:

   a. A climate action plan is put into place to reduce energy use and greenhouse gas emissions across the supply chain, and measures to achieve a goal based on science-based targets to achieve zero emissions by 2040.

   b. A waste-reduction plan is put in place with a goal of sending less to the landfill and instead recycling or repurposing all waste.

   c. A goal of reducing and eventually eliminating chemicals is created and all suppliers are asked to reduce toxic pesticides, dyes, finishes, etc.

   d. A target to reduce polluting/dumping wastewater into local waterways and works toward greater water efficiency.

   e. Programs put in place to protect against habitat loss, and to emphasize healthy habitat development and regeneration for all species of life and vegetation.

   f. An offset program is put in place to balance the negative impacts a company cannot reduce. Offsetting can include planting trees, investing in solar or wind, or other programs for natural carbon capture.

2. **Social**. In this area, profit is measured by social equity and justice programs implemented, and progress is shown in terms of fair labor practices, decent pay, and community development:

   a. A program is implemented to hire locally and pay a fair living wage that is equal to all regardless of race, gender, sexual orientation, and religion.

   b. A coffee-break project is launched that allows for worker breaks. Or there is a commitment made to break away from any factory that threatens workers, withholds pay for any reason, or forces more than 48 hours/per week.

   c. A program is put in place that contributes to training persons for jobs in the local workforce and/or that ensures all staff has access to health care.

   d. Space and staff for child care is provided for office and factory staff.

Table 9.1 Traditional Blank Cost Sheet with Eco-loading

Traditional Cost Sheet with Eco-Loading %					
Date		Company			
Style No.	Sxs No.	Season			Group
Size Range	Sxs Size	Description			
Fabric					
Fabric	**Est. Yield**	**@Est. $/yard**	**Est. Cost**	**Total Est. Cost**	**SKETCHES**
Fabric 1:					
Fabric 2:					
Freight:					
Trims	**Est. Quantity**	**@Est. $/ yard/gr/pc**	**Est. Cost**		
Trim 1:					
Trim 2:					
Trim 3:					
Freight:					**FRONT VIEW**
Notions	**Est. Quantity**	**@Est. $/ yard/gr/pc**	**Est. Cost**		
Notion 1:					
Notion 2:					
Freight:					
Labor	**Direct**	**Contract Work**			
Cutting:					
Sewing:					
Finishing:					
Marking/Grading:					
EST. First Cost of Goods					
Agent Commission %					
Est. Freight					
Duty %					
Clearance %					
Local Freight					
Product Development					
Factory Sourcing					**BACK VIEW**
Markdowns/Closeouts					
Eco-loading %					
Total Misc Costs					
Est. LDP / DDP Cost					
Wholesale Markup		Markup Goal %	100%–MU%	Markup $	
Wholesale Price					
Retailer Markup		Markup Goal %	100%–MU%	Markup $	
Retailer Price					
Manufacturer's Suggested Retail Price (MSRP)					

3. **Economical**. Lastly, profit is measured by how money is used to make life better for all in the communities where the business is located:

   a. A job growth program is implemented to add to the community's vibrant economic growth so money can flow and be exchanged in the places stakeholders live and work.

   b. Employees have enough wages to use for discretionary or pleasurable purchases, such as going to a movie theater.

   c. Reuse packaging, poly bags, boxes, and excess materials.

If we measure profit by how people's lives are improved in all the places that make our products, we can succeed. If we can measure earnings by the reduction of carbon dioxide being released into the air, customers will respond. Consideration of these factors can be used to create new business—doing and costing frameworks for our business where we work toward gain that is measured by how our actions in making product help improve the places and people who make our products.

An example is Puma. Puma is known to have worked with PricewaterhouseCoopers on their acclaimed Environmental Profit & Loss Statement (EP&L). They use this to compare, contrast, and learn to improve with each style. Puma's EP&L assigns dollar amounts to air and water pollution, GHG emissions, land change, and waste generation. By making these assessments visible to all, they have created a positive buzz that no amount of cost-cutting could create.

Convential Cotton Silk-Sreened Tee			Dry-Farmed Tee Digitally Printed		
Greenhouse Gas Emissions	$2.00		Greenhouse Gas Emissions	$1.50	
Energy Use	$0.75		Energy Use	$0.50	
Water Use	$1.00		Water Use	$0.30	
Waste and Landill	$0.50		Waste and Landill	$0.40	
Land Use	$0.40		Land Use	$0.35	
Chemical Use	$0.50		Chemical Use	$0.35	
TOTAL ENVIRONMENTAL COSTS	$5.15		TOTAL ENVIRONMENTAL COSTS	$3.40	
RETAIL SELLING PRICE	$30.00		RETAIL SELLING PRICE	$32.00	
ENVIRONMNETAL COSTS PERCENT OF RETAIL	17%		ENVIRONMNETAL COSTS PERCENT OF RETAIL	11%	

Here is a sketch of an EP&L statement example inspired by Puma. Here we look at the comparison in terms of costs to the planet of a conventionally grown cotton tee to a dry-farmed, no-till, regeneratively grown cotton tee.

Another innovative and sustainable clothing company is Mara Hoffman, where they prove you can balance what you spend in one area and offset dollars spent in another.

At the Mara Hoffman NYC design studio and showroom VP and Director of Sustainability Dana Davis advises, "We continuously strive to reduce our energy consumption in the office. On very bright days, we often work with the lights off and will keep windows open as far into the summer as possible until the air con is a must to keep us from physically melting."

This energy-saving action the company takes reduces their electric bill, and also helps to offset the costs of many of their responsible components, such as their compostable poly bags.

When a company wastes less, they are more economically responsible. The goal of a sustainably-minded company is to balance the three pillars—environmental, social, and economic—and make sure all are kept in mind as decisions are made. The more sustainable practices, the more revenue, which allows for greater cash flow. Just accessing and implementing sustainable practices helps a company become 51 percent more profitable or higher (Willard, 2017), and you need the cash flow and profit to continue the sustainable practices.

Additionally, companies can use the United Nations 17 Sustainable Development Goals (SDGs) as a guide. They can select one or two SDGs as a vision and create a plan and roadmap with measurable goals to help reach the SDGs. One company wanted to help work toward SDG 2–Zero Hunger, and they now host a bi-monthly dinner for all factory workers in their factory in India. Everyone gets a nutritious and balanced meal, and enjoys the camaraderie. Does the meal cost the brand more than not serving it at all? Yes, but their workers are certainly happy and feel appreciated, and quite possibly are more productive.

When workers are happy, employment turnover is reduced, and less time and money is spent training the newly employed. And that means less indirect cost factors.

It is important to cost your apparel with TBL practices, environmental and social programs, and SDG targets in mind. Sustainability in costing places a focus on ethically and socially responsible production, waste reduction, energy-efficiency, and transparency so that those factors show on cost sheet. The eco-loading percentage can vary from 2 to 5 percent per style for large companies, to 5 to 10 percent for smaller companies, but ultimately these costs can no longer be externalized. And if the eco-loading exceeds 10 percent, it is suggested the company work on educating their customers and telling the story of what they are doing to better the planet and combat social and environmental injustices. Companies should use engaging stories and visuals to explain the good programs and initiatives their prices include. The brands plan, assess, manage, and oversee corporate sustainability programs, however when they add a percent for sustainability to their pricing then the customers also become responsible for the good that is being done.

As earth's citizens, we need to work toward reducing natural resource abuse and creating a fossil-fuel-free environment when possible. Therefore, when we discuss selecting a synthetic fiber over a natural one in "Ways To Reduce Costs," that is the old way—the new way is consider that polyester is derived from petroleum, which is extracted from the earth and then melted and extruded to create the fiber. These processes emit large quantities of carbon dioxide into our atmosphere, and therefore contribute heavily to climate change. So in negotiating and watering down our styling to reduce costs, we are often increasing our externalized costs.

We are the *fashion* industry, we are creative, and we need to cost garments so our businesses can prosper, but we also must be open to change as the world changes. The world is changing, so please keep your pencils sharp, but keep your hearts open. Please spend as much time pondering over beautiful details and gorgeous shapes as you do with every line on your cost sheets.

Sustainably-run companies recognize that their businesses are interconnected with all people and the entire planet. Creating a line with no impact might not look right on our cost sheets, as we cannot measure human worth like we can three yards of fabric; but as an industry, we must consider the earth and the people, as well as our customers. *And our customers* do care about our planet and are concerned with its future. Our customers have no interest in our indirect costs, overhead percents, and SAMs. Perhaps we can visualize how we can creatively design and bring a fashionable and responsible product to market. Remembering every cost, internal and external, in creating fashion is the right thing to do—for the planet, for our companies, for our customers, and, in the end, for our bottom lines.

Blockchain Technology

As customers demand more transparency from the brands they know and love, blockchain technology is proving to be a viable solution, offering a new paradigm of data sharing/management from fiber to final garment. Current information systems such PLM and WebPDM offer connectivity between designers, buyers, manufacturers, and stakeholders along the value chain, but they are only available if each actor has the technology and infrastructure to adopt uniform systems.

Blockchain has similar challenges to other information systems, but its value proposition is in its distributed data storage. Blockchain aims to usher in a new era of peer to peer, real-time data sharing, where data is authenticated in a way that does not require transacting parties to trust each other. This trustless system can support transparent supply chains because once information is uploaded to the system, it is essentially impossible to alter. So should transacting parties along a supply chain wish to embrace transparency, they can trust that other actors are held to the same standards. Blockchain offers hope to provide more customers with information, but it still requires brands to allow customers access to the information. Without significant buy-in from all stakeholders along the supply chain, blockchain remains an industry tool; however, it has the power to evolve into a great consumer tool to help increase brand loyalty, trust, and transparency from farmer to consumer.

Summary

A line item must be added to our cost sheets that covers not only our doing-business-as-usual costs, but our costs to produce positively on this earth. Planet Earth and those who live here are affected by unsustainable practices. In designing with sustainability in mind, companies reduce their negative impact and satisfy their ever-wiser customer base.

Eco-loading is the process of logging all expenditures made in the name of sustainability. While the cost may initially seem like a liability, measures taken toward sustainability are often met with success in the form of profits, as well.

Success can be measured not just in profits but in impact. There are three main ways we measure impact: environmental, social, and economical. If we measure profit by how people's lives are improved in all the places that make our products and by how much carbon dioxide is reduced, we can succeed and so can the customers and the manufacturers. We all want a great product that breaks the mold, not the bank or the planet. Please consider sustainability in all items you cost going forward.

Chapter Review and Discussion

1. What is an eco-loading percent? Why are some companies loading these costs onto their cost sheets?
2. How would you explain sustainability in costing to a grandparent?
3. How does the eco-loading percent change depending on the size of one's business? Why?
4. The Levi Strauss Co. has been applauded for its exciting "100 by 25" plan. This means they have a goal to use 100 percent renewable energy by 2025 on all Levis-owned properties. Their prices have risen by just pennies per style. Why is this?

Activities and Exercises

1. Imagine you own a dress company and want to empower women and girls. You decide to create a program using SDG 5–Gender Equality as a framework. What is a program you can introduce to help one of your stakeholders? Who is the program geared to? What would it involve? What cost impacts would it have? How would you track and measure its success?

2. Research offset programs that businesses can join. How much do they cost? Per month? Per year? Imagine you produce roughly 9,000 styles/season and the average retail price is $55. What would your eco-loading percent be if you started this offset program for one season?

Key Terms

eco-loading

Glossary

activity-based costing: A costing method that assigns a monetary value to each and every production activity and overhead expense.

actual cost: The evaluation and determination of the cost of a style or styles after the order is produced, shipped, and sold. Also known as post-production costing.

bill of labor (BOL): Document listing separate activities but the number of minutes or hours.

bill of materials (BOM): Detailed list of all fabric, trims, finding, and other materials that are included in the production of a style and list of the supplier name and all fiber details, etc. A BOM is required for each colorway and should include the same materials as the cost sheet

bottom line: A company's total net profit (earnings) in terms of dollars, over a certain period of time. The bottom line is the last (bottom) line on an income statement.

break bulk: Separation of large order to be distributed to multiple retailers

chargeback: A percent or dollar amount deducted by the retailer/vendor from the wholesaler/manufacturer's invoice when an order is received incomplete, late, or not as precisely specified by the retailer/vendor in advance.

CIF (cost, insurance, and freight): The cost of the goods to be manufactured, delivered to the port or loading dock, uploaded to the ship, plane or truck, and shipped, with all applicable insurance fees included along the way. The cost does not include duties, clearing customs, or local shipping. The responsibility of the manufacturer of the goods ends at when the goods arrive at the destination port.

CM (cut and make): This is a garment-production term and is the cost for the garments/items to be cut and sewn. This is a labor-only price and does not include pattern making, materials, tagging, packing, shipping, or taxes. The responsibility of the factory is only to make the goods.

CMT (cut, make, and trim): This is a garment-production term and is the cost for the garments/items to be cut, sewn, trimmed, tagged/labeled, and inspected. This price generally does not include patternmaking and materials (but at times does) nor shipping or taxes.

CMTP (Cut, Make, Trim, and Pack): This is a garment-production term and is the cost for the garments/items to be cut, sewn, trimmed, tagged/labeled, inspected and packed. This price generally does not include patternmaking and materials (but at times does) nor shipping or taxes.

COGS (cost of goods): Material and labor costs associated with a garment or group of garments.

competitive pricing: Price strategy where product price is set to meet the competitions price.

COO (country of origin): The country in which the goods were sewn in.

cost estimating: An estimate of costs early in the development stage. Also known as pre-production costing, sample costing, pre-costing, and/or predictive costing.

DDP (delivered and duty paid): The cost of the goods to be manufactured, delivered to the port/loading dock, uploaded to the vessel, shipped, insured, offloaded from the vessel, brought through customs, with duties/paid loaded on to a local forwarder, and delivered to your warehouse/retailer/etc. The cost includes everything up until the goods arrive at your door.

demographics: Customer characteristics such as gender, age, marital status, and education.

determined cost: The cost based on the manufacturing a style once the style details are finalized and the fabric, trimming, and labor costs are known. Also known as production costing, final cost, or standard cost, and includes overhead, transportation costs, and duties and customs clearance.

direct cost: The sum of the price of the fabric, lining, trims, notions, pattern, and all required direct labor (also known as first cost).

direct sourcing: Traveling overseas, visiting factories and suppliers oneself.

direct-to-consumer: Manufacturers sell directly to consumer.

discount: A percent or dollar amount the retailer deducts from the full price of merchandise when a customer makes a purchase using a coupon or employee, military, frequent-buyer, or any other discount offer.

duty (tariffs): Taxes imposed on goods produced outside of the home country.

eco-loading: The practice of adding a percent to cover sustainability and ethical production that is added to a cost sheet

Enterprise Resource Planning (ERP) Software used to help manufacturers have share and access information throughout the development and production of a style

everyday low pricing: Price strategy where products are set at a low price and consistently remain at a low price.

ExW (Ex-Works): The cost of the goods to be manufactured. Price does not include handling, shipping, or taxes. The responsibility of the manufacturer of the goods ends at the factory outgoing door (also known as X-FTY or Ex-Factory).

fabric consumption: The amount of fabric required per yard or meter it takes to produce one style (also known as fabric yield).

fabric yield: The amount of fabric required per yard or meter it takes to produce one style. (also known as fabric consumption)

FAS (free alongside): The cost of the goods to be manufactured and delivered to the port, loading dock, etc. The cost does not include uploading to the ship, plane or truck, shipping, or taxes. The responsibility of the manufacturer of the goods ends at when it is delivered to the shipper.

fashion items: Products which are trendy or have a shorter selling cycle.

final cost: The cost based on the manufacturing a style once the style details are finalized and the fabric, trimming, and labor costs are known. Also known as production costing, standard cost, or determined cost and includes overhead, transportation costs, and duties and customs clearance.

first cost: The sum of the price of the fabric, lining, trims, notions, pattern, and all required direct labor (also known as direct cost).

fixed costs: Costs that remain unchanged from month to month or order to order.

FOB (free on board): The cost of the goods to be manufactured, delivered to the port or loading dock, and uploaded to the ship, plane, or truck. The cost does not include shipping or taxes. The responsibility of the manufacturer of the goods ends when the goods are loaded onto the shipping vessel.

FPP (full package production): This is a garment-production term and is the cost for the garments/items to be cut, sewn, trimmed, tagged/labeled, inspected, and packed, and includes patternmaking, sampling, and purchasing of raw materials. This price does not include shipping or taxes.

freight forwarder: Someone who organizes transportation of goods

geographics: Customer characteristics related to geographic location

high-low pricing: Price strategy where product price is first set high and reduced to incentive customers to buy on sale.

Incidentals: Unforeseen increases in expenses

income statement: A company's financial performance over a certain period of time. Generally an income statement is one page and includes total sales revenue and income, less cost of goods, taxes, and operating and other expenses to arrive at the net profit (or loss) for the specified period.

Incoterms®: Universal terms used in manufacturing, importing, and exporting that define the responsibilities of sellers and buyers for the delivery of goods under contract; published by the International Chamber of Commerce (ICC). Search the ICCWBO website for further details on Incoterms®.

indirect costs: Related procedures, activities, and expenses that benefit all styles created and are necessary for the business to operate.

keystone: Marking up an item at twice the produced or purchased cost.

lab dips Approval samples for fabrics and trims used for color matching and quality and weight testing.

landed Shipment that has cleared customs.

LDP (landed and duty paid): The cost of the goods to be manufactured, delivered to the port/ loading dock, uploaded to the vessel, shipped, insured, offloaded from the vessel, and brought through customs, with all duties/ paid.

list price: The price at which a wholesaler recommends that retailers sell their product. Also known as the suggested retail price (SRP), manufacturer's suggested retail price (MSRP), or recommended retail price.

manufacturer's suggested retail price (MSRP): The price at which a wholesaler recommends that retailers sell their product. Also known as the suggested retail price (SRP), recommended retail price, or list price.

markdown: A percent or dollar amount the retailer discounts merchandise when it is unable to be unsold at full price. Markdowns may be applied to help sell product received incomplete, late, damaged, or not found desirable by the customer.

markup percent: Difference between cost and retail divided by cost.

omni-channel: Brand selecting all channels of distribution to sell goods.

overhead: Business expenses not directly associated with the creation of product, but exist so business can operate.

overhead percent: Relationship between indirect and direct expenses. Indirect expenses divided by the direct expenses.

penetration pricing: Price strategy where products are set at a lower price and markup with a goal of high sales volume.

perception map: Research tool used to identify gaps in the market and/or competitors.

PLM (Product Lifecycle Management): Software that manages the information of a style through design, development, material procurement, production, and distribution.

point of measure: Specific points along the body that are used to determine the pattern, sizes, and fit of the garment.

POS system (point of sales): Any device that completes a purchase.

post-production costing: The evaluation and determination of the actual cost of a style or styles after the order is produced, shipped, and sold. Also known as actual cost.

pre-costing: A preliminary estimate of costs early in the development stage. Also known as pre- production costing, sample costing, cost estimating, and/or predictive costing.

pre-production costing: A preliminary estimate of costs early in the development stage. Also known as sample costing, pre-costing, cost estimating, and/or predictive costing.

predictive costing: A preliminary estimate of costs early in the development stage. Also known as pre- production costing, sample costing, pre-costing, and/or cost estimating.

premium pricing: See status pricing.

price point: Target price for a product.

pricing range: Brands consistent price range.

private label: When a large retailer cuts out the middleman or the wholesaler and works with the manufacturer to develop its own line.

production costing: The cost based on the manufacturing a style once the style details are finalized and the fabric, trimming, and labor costs are known. Also known as final cost, standard cost, or determined cost and includes overhead, transportation costs, duties and customs clearance.

profit: the amount of money gained; the difference between the amount spent and earned after selling).

profit margin: The percent of the selling price that becomes the profit.

psychographics: Customer characteristics related to a customer's hobbies or interests.

recommended retail price: The price at which a wholesaler recommends that retailers sell their product. Also known as the suggested retail price (SRP), manufacturer's suggested retail price (MSRP), or list price.

sample costing: A preliminary estimate of costs early in the development stage that is performed when samples are produced. Also known as pre-production costing, pre-costing, cost estimating, and/or predictive costing.

self-fabric: When the fabrication used for a lining or trim (i.e., to cover buttons or piping) is the same fabric that is used for the exterior or body of the garment.

SKU (stock keeping unit): The smallest unit of measure when referring to a style. A SKU is generally the amount of colors multiplied by the amount of sizes in a style.

sloper: A basic paper pattern which when cut and sewn will cover a three-dimensional surface.

sourcing agent: Organizes sourcing, procuring materials, and securing production factories.

standard allowed minutes (SAMs): Measurement used to calculate and communicate amount of time an activity takes to complete in minutes.

standard cost: The cost based on the manufacturing a style once the style details are finalized and the fabric, trimming, and labor costs are known. Also known as production costing, final cost, or determined cost, and includes overhead, transportation costs, and duties and customs clearance.

staple items: Products that do not go out of style and remain a core component of a collection.

status pricing: Price strategy where products are set at a high price creating a perception of value by the customers.

suggested retail price (SRP): The price at which a manufacturer/wholesaler recommends that retailers sell their product. Also known as the manufacturer's suggested retail price (MSRP), recommended retail price, or list price.

target cost: The expected, and maximum allowable, total cost of a garment/product based on a selling price you believe your customer will pay.

target customer: The person or group a company is selling to.

technical package: A detailed set of written and illustrated garment specifications for a style so that it can be produced.

top line: A company's total gross sales or revenue in terms of dollars, over a certain period of time. The top line is the first (top) line on an income statement.

US Harmonized Tariff Schedule List of duty rates categorized by product characteristics created by the United States International Trade Commission.

value: The relationship between price and quality.

value-based costing: Working backwards from the selling price to determine an approximate cost of an item.

variable costs: Costs that differ depending on the season and order size, as well as on the complexity of the styles and products being produced.

white space: Gaps in the market often leading to market opportunity.

wholesale price: The cost of a product sold by a wholesaler to a retailer for resale.

X-FTY (Ex-Factory): The cost of the goods to be manufactured. Price does not include handling, shipping, or taxes. The responsibility of the manufacturer of the goods ends at the factory outgoing door (also known as ExW or Ex-Works).

References

Apparel Costing (2017), "What is the Meaning of SMV? | SMV of Different Apparel", © *Apparel Costing blog spot*, June. Available online: https://apparelcosting.blogspot.com/2017/06/standard-minute-value-sam-smv-industrial-engineering.html (accessed October 2019).

Asia Floor Wage Alliance (2017), "Asia Floor Wage What is it and why do we need one?", *AFWA*. Available online: https://asia.floorwage.org/what (accessed October 2019).

Baldwin, Cory (2017), "Here's How Much It Actually Costs to Make Your Shirt", *Racked*, 6 January. Available online: https://www.racked.com/2017/1/6/14157836/elizabeth-suzann-money-talk (accessed October 2019).

Belgum, D. (2018), "Tariffs on China Could Broadly Affect Clothing and Footwear Imports", *California Apparel News*, 22 March. Available online: https://www.apparelnews.net/news/2018/mar/22/tariffs-china-could-broadly-affect-clothing-and-fo/ (accessed October 2019).

Birnbaum, D. (2008), "Birnbaum's Global Guide to Winning the Great Garment War", *Birnbaum Garment*, 1 July. Available online: http://www.birnbaumgarment.com/2008/07/01/birnbaums-global-guide-to-winning-the-garment-war/ (accessed October 2019).

Blum, K. (2018), "Questions about Customs Broker fees for new textbook: The Apparel Costing Workbook", *Email*.

Coats (2014), "Thread Consumption Guide", *Coats Group plc*, November. Available online: https://www.coats.com/en/Information-Hub/The-Guide-to-Thread-Consumption (accessed October 2019).

Creglia-Atwi, J. (2018) Phone conversation and email with author Andrea Kennedy.

Hughes, A. (2005), "ABC/ABM – activity-based costing and activity-based management", *Journal of Fashion Marketing and Management*, Vol. 9 No. 1, pp. 8–19. 1 March. Available online: https://doi.org/10.1108/13612020510586370 (accessed October 2019).

Kennedy, A. (2017), "On Creating Right-Brained Fashion", *The Fashion Studies Journal*, 6 May. Available online: http://www.fashionstudiesjournal.org/notes/2017/6/6/on-creating-right-brained-fashion?fbclid=IwAR2Pn4b9pfXlTgxzlro5EhFUbnRr-0q_T7QfF2aBrBAV2BpyAvoziQGy3vY (accessed October 2019).

Lu, Sheng (2018), "Wage Level for Garment Workers in the World (updated in 2017)", *Sheng Lu Fashion*, 4 March. Available online: https://shenglufashion.com/2018/03/04/wage-level-for-garment-workers-in-the-world-updated-in-2017/ (accessed October 2019).

Mui, Ylan Q. and Rosenwald, Michael S. (2008), "Wal-Mart Shelves Old Slogan After 19 Years", *Washington Post*, 28 March, updated 25 May 2011. Available online: https://www.huffingtonpost.com/2007/09/13/walmart-shelves-old-sloga_n_64289.html (accessed October 2019).

Nayeem Emran, S. and Kyriacou, Joy. (2017), "What She Make, Power and Poverty in the Fashion Industry", *Oxfam Australia*, October. Available online: http://whatshemakes.oxfam.org.au/wp-content/uploads/2017/10/Living-Wage-Media-Report_WEB.pdf (accessed October 2019).

Noah, David (2017), "Freight Forwarder Pricing: What Are These Extra Fees on My Invoice?", *Shipping Solutions*, 6 December. Available online: https://www.shippingsolutions.com/blog/freight-forwarder-pricing (accessed October 2019).

Reagan, Courtney (2018), "You're already paying tariffs on clothing and shoes, and have been for almost 90 years", *CNBC*, updated 6 April. Available online: https://www.cnbc.com/2018/04/06/americans-are-already-paying-tariffs-on-clothing-and-shoes.html (accessed October 2019).

Sarkar, Prasanta (2011), "Standard Minutes (SAM or SMV) for Few Basic Garment Products", *Online Clothing Study*, 25 September. Available online: https://www.onlineclothingstudy.com/2011/09/standard-minutes-sam-or-smv-for-few.html (accessed October 2019).

Talekar, Sunil (2014), "Line Balancing", © *SOFT Student Handouts*, 3 January. Available online: https://www.slideshare.net/suniltalekar1/7-line-balancing-i-apparel-industry (accessed October 2019).

Tuovila, Alicia (2019), "Bottom Line", *Investopedia*, 9 August. Available online: https://www.investopedia.com/terms/b/bottomline.asp (accessed October 2019).

Companion Website Resources

Online resources to accompany this book are available at: www.bloomsbury.com/cw/apparel-costing. Please type the URL into your web browser and follow the instructions to access the Companion Website. If you experience any problems, please contact Bloomsbury at: companionwebsites@bloomsbury.com.

The costing companion website offers additional tools to support you in sharpening your costing skills, as well as challenging you to think critically about costing and pricing. The site includes free-to-download sample cost sheets, the end of chapter questions and activities included in this book, and further multiple-choice assessment questions, all arranged by chapter to help you become adept at costing fashion garments and all types of clothing and accessories.

Sample Cost Sheets

Basic Cost Sheet					
Date		Company			
Style No.	Sxs No.	Season			Group
Size Range	Sxs Size	Description			
Fabric					
Fabric	Est. Yield	@Est. $/yard	Est. Cost	Total Est. Cost	SKETCHES
Fabric 1:					
Fabric 2:					
Freight:					
Trims	Est. Quantity	@Est. $/ yard/gr/pc	Est. Cost		
Trim 1:					
Trim 2:					
Trim 3:					FRONT VIEW
Freight:					
Notions	Est. Quantity	@Est. $/ yard/gr/pc	Est. Cost		
Notion 1:					
Notion 2:					
Freight:					
Labor	Direct	Contract Work			
Cutting:					
Sewing:					
Finishing:					
Marking/Grading:					
EST. First Cost of Goods					
		Markup Goal %	100% - MU%	Markup $	
Selling Price					
					BACK VIEW

Bill of Labor						
Date			Company			
Style No.		Sxs No.	Season			Group
Size Range		Sxs Size	Description			
Description	Type	Base Rate	SAMs	Total Time	Cost (Time x Rate)	STYLE SKETCH
				TOTAL TIME	TOTAL BOL COST	

Bill of Labor Sheet with Common Labor Activities						
Date			**Company**			
Style No.		**Sxs No.**	**Season**			**Group**
Size Range		**Sxs Size**	**Description**			
Description	**Type**	**Base Rate**	**SAMs**	**Total Time**	**Cost (Time x Rate)**	**STYLE SKETCH**
Cutting						
Fusing						
Bundling						
Sewing—Shell						
Sewing—Lining						
Sewing—Other						
Serging						
Seam Finishes—Other						
Topstitch						
Stitching—Other						
Buttons						
Buttonholes						
Notions—Other						
Pressing						
Applique						
Embroidery						
Trim Application						
Hems						
Snipping						
Finishing						
Steaming						
Pressing						
Inspection						
Tagging						
Folding						
Hanging						
Bagging						
Packing						
				TOTAL TIME	**TOTAL BOL COST**	

Bill of Materials						
Date			Company			
Style No.		Sxs No.	Season			Group
Size Range		Sxs Size	Description			
Material and Description	Placement	Yield or Quantity	@ $/ yard/gr/pc	Country of Origin	Total Cost	STYLE SKETCH
				GRAND TOTAL COST	

Overhead Cost Tracking Sheet	
Company	
Date	
Description	**Total Costs**
Office/Showroom Space	
Warehouse Space	
Material Handling	
Equipment/Machinery	
Equipment/Machinery Maintenance	
Office/Showroom Furnishings	
Office/Showroom Supplies	
Salaries	
Commissions	
Utilities	
Web Services	
Meals/Entertainment	
Gifts	
Carfare	
Advertising/Marketing	
Shipping Costs	
Accounting Fees	
Legal Fees	
Insurance	
Losses Due to Theft	
Other	
Grand Total Overhead Costs	

Private Label Retailer Cost Sheet					
Date		Company			
Style No.	Sxs No.	Season			Group
Size Range	Sxs Size	Description			
Fabric					
Fabric	Est. Yield	@Est. $/ yard	Est. Cost	Total Est. Cost	SKETCHES
Fabric 1:					
Fabric 2:					
Freight:					
Trims	Est. Quantity	@Est. $/ yard/gr/pc	Est. Cost		
Trim 1:					
Trim 2:					
Trim 3:					
Freight:					FRONT VIEW
Notions	Est. Quantity	@Est. $/ yard/gr/pc	Est. Cost		
Notion 1:					
Notion 2:					
Freight:					
Labor	Direct	Contract Work			
Cutting:					
Sewing:					
Finishing:					
Marking/Grading:					
EST. First Cost of Goods					
Agent Commission %					
Est. Freight					
Duty %					BACK VIEW
Clearance %					
Local Freight					
Product Development Costs					
Total Misc Costs					
Est. LDP / DDP Cost					
Private Label Retailer Markup	Markup Goal %	100% - MU%	Markup $		
Private Label Retailer Price					
Manufacturer's Suggested Retail Price (MSRP)					

Production Cost Sheet					
Date		**Company**			
Style No.	**Sxs No.**	**Season**			**Group**
Size Range	**Sxs Size**	**Description**			
Fabric					
Fabric	**Yield/Style**	**Cost/Yard**	**Cost/Garment**	**Total/Garment**	**SKETCHES**
Fabric 1:					
Fabric 2:					
Fabric 3:					
Freight:					
Trims	**Yield/Style**	**Cost/ Yard/ Gr/Pc**	**Cost/Garment**	**Total/Garment**	
Trim 1:					
Trim 2:					
Trim 3:					
Freight:					**FRONT VIEW**
Notions	**Yield/Style**	**Cost/ Yard/ Gr/Pc**	**Cost/Garment**	**Total/Garment**	
Notion 1:					
Notion 2:					
Notion 3:					
Freight:					
Labor	**Country**	**Direct Labor**	**Contract Work**	**Total/Garment**	
Cutting					
Sewing					
Finishing					
Marking/Grading					
Cost of Goods					
Agent Commission %					
Freight					
Duty %					**BACK VIEW**
Clearance %					
Local Freight					
LDP / DDP Cost					
	A	**B**	**C**	**D**	
Sell Price					
Net Profit (Sell Price less Cost)					
Net Profit % (Net Profit div by Sell)					

ONE TIME START UP EXPENSES		AMOUNT		NOTES
One Time Start-Up Costs:				
Rent Deposit				
Furniture & Fixtures				
Equipment				
Buildout/ Renovations				
Decorating, Painting and Remodeling				
Installation of Fixtures & Equipment				
Starting Inventory				
Deposits with Public Utilities				
Legal and Other Professional Fees				
License and Permits				
Advertising and Promotion				
Consulting				
Software				
Cash				
Other:				
Other:				
Other:				
Other:				
Total One Time Start-Up Costs:				
Monthly Expenses:				
Bank Charges				
Debt Service (Principal & Interest)				
Insurance				
Membership & Dues				
Maintenance & Repairs				
Marketing & Promotion: Advertising				
Marketing & Promotion: Other				
Miscellaneous				
Payroll: Wages (Owner/ Manager)				
Payroll: Wages (Employees)				
Payroll Tax				
Professional Fees: Accounting				
Professional Fees: Legal				
Professional Fees: Other				
Rent				
Subscriptions				
Supplies: Office				
Supplies: Operating				
Telephone				
Utilities				
Other:				
Total Monthly Expenses:				
Number of months required to cover Expenses:				Working Capital
TOTAL START-UP FUNDS REQUIRED:				
Loan Amount (At 80% of Total Start-Up)				

Traditional Cost Sheet with Eco-Loading %					
Date		Company			
Style No.	Sxs No.	Season			Group
Size Range	Sxs Size	Description			
Fabric					
Fabric	**Est. Yield**	**@Est. $/yard**	**Est. Cost**	**Total Est. Cost**	**SKETCHES**
Fabric 1:					
Fabric 2:					
Freight:					
Trims	**Est. Quantity**	**@Est. $/ yard/gr/pc**	**Est. Cost**		
Trim 1:					
Trim 2:					
Trim 3:					
Freight:					**FRONT VIEW**
Notions	**Est. Quantity**	**@Est. $/ yard/gr/pc**	**Est. Cost**		
Notion 1:					
Notion 2:					
Freight:					
Labor	**Direct**	**Contract Work**			
Cutting:					
Sewing:					
Finishing:					
Marking/Grading:					
EST. First Cost of Goods					
Agent Commission %					
Est. Freight					
Duty %					
Clearance %					
Local Freight					
Product Development					
Factory Sourcing					**BACK VIEW**
Markdowns/Closeouts					
Eco-loading %					
Total Misc Costs					
Est. LDP / DDP Cost					
Wholesale Markup		**Markup Goal %**	**100% - MU%**	**Markup $**	
Wholesale Price					
Retailer Markup		**Markup Goal %**	**100% - MU%**	**Markup $**	
Retailer Price					
Manufacturer's Suggested Retail Price (MSRP)					

Traditional Cost Sheet with Global Sourcing					
Date		Company			
Style No.	Sxs No.	Season			Group
Size Range	Sxs Size	Description			
Fabric					
Fabric	**Est. Yield**	**@Est. $/yard**	**Est. Cost**	**Total Est. Cost**	**SKETCHES**
Fabric 1:					
Fabric 2:					
Freight:					
Trims	**Est. Quantity**	**@Est. $/ yard/gr/pc**	**Est. Cost**		
Trim 1:					
Trim 2:					
Trim 3:					
Freight:					**FRONT VIEW**
Notions	**Est. Quantity**	**@Est. $/ yard/gr/pc**	**Est. Cost**		
Notion 1:					
Notion 2:					
Freight:					
Labor	**Direct**	**Contract Work**			
Cutting:					
Sewing:					
Finishing:					
Marking/Grading:					
EST. First Cost of Goods					
Agent Commission %					
Factory Sourcing					
Est. Freight					
Duty %					
Clearance %					**BACK VIEW**
Local Freight					
Total Misc Costs					
Est. LDP / DDP Cost					
Wholesale Markup		Markup Goal %	100% - MU%	Markup $	
Wholesale Price					
Retailer Markup		Markup Goal %	100% - MU%	Markup $	
Retailer Price					
Manufacturer's Suggested Retail Price (MSRP)					

Traditional Cost Sheet					
Date		Company			
Style No.	Sxs No.	Season			Group
Size Range	Sxs Size	Description			
Fabric					
Fabric	Est. Yield	@Est. $/yard	Est. Cost	Total Est. Cost	SKETCHES
Fabric 1:					
Fabric 2:					
Freight:					
Trims	Est. Quantity	@Est. $/ yard/gr/pc	Est. Cost		
Trim 1:					
Trim 2:					
Trim 3:					
Freight:					FRONT VIEW
Notions	Est. Quantity	@Est. $/ yard/gr/pc	Est. Cost		
Notion 1:					
Notion 2:					
Freight:					
Labor	Direct	Contract Work			
Cutting:					
Sewing:					
Finishing:					
Marking/Grading:					
EST. First Cost of Goods					
Agent Commission %					
Est. Freight					
Duty %					
Clearance %					
Local Freight					BACK VIEW
Markdowns / Closeouts					
Total Misc Costs					
Est. LDP / DDP Cost					
Wholesale Markup		Markup Goal %	100% - MU%	Markup $	
Wholesale Price					
Retailer Markup		Markup Goal %	100% - MU%	Markup $	
Retailer Price					
Manufacturer's Suggested Retail Price (MSRP)					

Traditional Cost Sheet with PD Loading					
Date		Company			
Style No.	Sxs No.	Season			Group
Size Range	Sxs Size	Description			
Fabric					
Fabric	Est. Yield	@Est. $/yard	Est. Cost	Total Est. Cost	SKETCHES
Fabric 1:					
Fabric 2:					
Freight:					
Trims	Est. Quantity	@Est. $/ yard/gr/pc	Est. Cost		
Trim 1:					
Trim 2:					
Trim 3:					
Freight:					FRONT VIEW
Notions	Est. Quantity	@Est. $/ yard/gr/pc	Est. Cost		
Notion 1:					
Notion 2:					
Freight:					
Labor	Direct	Contract Work			
Cutting:					
Sewing:					
Finishing:					
Marking/Grading:					
EST. First Cost of Goods					
Agent Commission %					
Est. Freight					
Duty %					
Clearance %					
Local Freight					BACK VIEW
Product Development					
Total Misc Costs					
Est. LDP / DDP Cost					
Wholesale Markup		Markup Goal %	100% - MU%	Markup $	
Wholesale Price					
Retailer Markup		Markup Goal %	100% - MU%	Markup $	
Retailer Price					
Manufacturer's Suggested Retail Price (MSRP)					

Traditional Cost Sheet					
Date		Company			
Style No.	Sxs No.	Season			Group
Size Range	Sxs Size	Description			
Fabric					
Fabric	**Est. Yield**	**@Est. $/yard**	**Est. Cost**	**Total Est. Cost**	**SKETCHES**
Fabric 1:					
Fabric 2:					
Freight:					
Trims	**Est. Quantity**	**@Est. $/ yard/gr/pc**	**Est. Cost**		
Trim 1:					
Trim 2:					
Trim 3:					
Freight:					**FRONT VIEW**
Notions	**Est. Quantity**	**@Est. $/ yard/gr/pc**	**Est. Cost**		
Notion 1:					
Notion 2:					
Freight:					
Labor	**Direct**	**Contract Work**			
Cutting:					
Sewing:					
Finishing:					
Marking/Grading:					
EST. First Cost of Goods					
Agent Commission %					
Est. Freight					
Duty %					
Clearance %					
Local Freight					**BACK VIEW**
Total Misc Costs					
Est. LDP / DDP Cost					
Wholesale Markup		Markup Goal %	100% - MU%	Markup $	
Wholesale Price					
Retailer Markup		Markup Goal %	100% - MU%	Markup $	
Retailer Price					
Manufacturer's Suggested Retail Price (MSRP)					

Index

9 781350 065406